Ninja Foodi 2-Basket Air Fryer Cookbook for Beginners

1000-Days Easy & Delicious Recipes for Beginners and Advanced Users. Easier, Healthier, & Crispier Food for Your Family & Friends

Julia Adamo

TABLE OF CONTENTS

Introduction

Do you really want to reduce your kitchen time? Do you want to prepare two different meals at one time? Then grab the Ninja Foodi Dual Zone Air fryer and Air fry all your favorite meals in its two cooking chambers. This smart Air fryer is specially designed with the amazing dual-zone technology that will help you cook two different meals at a time or a single meal in large portions using smart finish or match cooking technology. That's right! Ninja Kitchen has made it possible.

The Ninja dual Air fryer has a total of 8 qt capacity, which is divided into two 4qt cooking zones- Zone 1 and Zone 2. The number of the zone is given on the air fryer baskets so you could easily detect them. Each zone has a portion in the display, and it shows their respective settings. You can use the respective keys to set the time and temperature for each zone. There are some other smart features of this dual appliance that you can use to cook all your meals with convenience:

The Smart Finish Function

The smart finish can help you cook different things in each cooking zone at different temperatures and times. When you press this button, you can select the temperature and time for each zone separately.

The "MATCH COOK" Technology

Let's say you want to cook meals in both of its air frying baskets at the same temperature and for the same time duration. You can then use the "MATCH COOK" option. To do so, you will first need to:

- Select the cooking mode, temperature, and time for Zone 1
- Then press the "MATCH COOK" function to copy these settings for zone 2.
- Now both the zone will have the same settings.
- After pressing the START button, they will start preheating and cooking the food in their respective chambers.

It's about time that you give this appliance a try and do some cooking!

Breakfast Recipes

Morning Patties

Prep Time: 15 minutes.
Cook Time: 13 minutes.
Serves: 4

Ingredients:

- 1 lb minced pork
- 1 lb minced turkey
- 2 teaspoons dry rubbed sage
- 2 teaspoons fennel seeds
- 2 teaspoons garlic powder
- 1 teaspoon paprika
- 1 teaspoon of sea salt
- 1 teaspoon dried thyme

Preparation:

1. In a mixing bowl, add turkey and pork, then mix them together.
2. Mix sage, fennel, paprika, salt, thyme, and garlic powder in a small bowl.
3. Drizzle this mixture over the meat mixture and mix well.
4. Take 2 tablespoons of this mixture at a time and roll it into thick patties.
5. Place half of the patties in Basket 1, and the other half in basket 2, then spray them all with cooking oil.
6. Return the Air Fryer Baskets to the Air Fryer.
7. Choose the Air Fryer mode for Zone 1 with 390 degrees F temperature and 13 minutes cooking time.
8. Select the "MATCH COOK" option to copy the settings for Zone 2.
9. Initiate cooking by pressing the START/PAUSE BUTTON.
10. Flip the patties in the baskets once cooked halfway through.
11. Serve warm and fresh.

Serving Suggestion: Serve the patties with toasted bread slices.

Variation Tip: Ground chicken or beef can also be used instead of ground pork and turkey.

Nutritional Information Per Serving:

Calories 305 | Fat 25g |Sodium 532mg | Carbs 2.3g | Fiber 0.4g | Sugar 2g | Protein 18.3g

Crispy Hash Browns

Prep Time: 10 minutes.
Cook Time: 13 minutes.
Serves: 4

Ingredients:

- 3 russet potatoes
- ¼ cup chopped green peppers
- ¼ cup chopped red peppers
- ¼ cup chopped onions
- 2 garlic cloves chopped
- 1 teaspoon paprika
- Salt and black pepper, to taste
- 2 teaspoons olive oil

Preparation:

1. Peel and grate all the potatoes with the help of a cheese grater.
2. Add potato shreds to a bowl filled with cold water and leave it soaked for 25 minutes.
3. Drain the water and place the potato shreds on a plate lined with a paper towel.
4. Transfer the shreds to a dry bowl and add olive oil, paprika, garlic, and black pepper.
5. Make four flat patties out of the potato mixture and place two into each of the Air fryer baskets.
6. Return the Air Fryer Baskets to the Air Fryer.
7. Choose the Air Fryer mode for Zone 1 with 390 degrees F temperature and 13 minutes cooking time.
8. Select the "MATCH COOK" option to copy the settings for Zone 2.
9. Initiate cooking by pressing the START/PAUSE BUTTON.
10. Flip the potato hash browns once cooked halfway through, then resume cooking.
11. Once done, serve warm.

Serving Suggestion: Serve the hash with toasted bread slices and crispy bacon.

Variation Tip: Add herbed cream on top of the hash browns.

Nutritional Information Per Serving:
Calories 190 | Fat 18g |Sodium 150mg | Carbs 0.6g | Fiber 0.4g | Sugar 0.4g | Protein 7.2g

Air Fried Sausage

Prep Time: 10 minutes.
Cook Time: 13 minutes.
Serves: 4

Ingredients:

* 4 sausage links, raw and uncooked

Preparation:

1. Divide the sausages in the two Air fryer baskets.
2. Return the Air Fryer Baskets to the Air Fryer.
3. Choose the Air Fryer mode for Zone 1 with 390 degrees F temperature and 13 minutes cooking time.
4. Select the "MATCH COOK" option to copy the settings for Zone 2.
5. Initiate cooking by pressing the START/PAUSE BUTTON.
6. Serve warm and fresh.

Serving Suggestion: Serve the sausages with toasted bread and eggs.

Variation Tip: Add black pepper and salt for seasoning.

Nutritional Information Per Serving:
Calories 267 | Fat 12g |Sodium 165mg | Carbs 39g | Fiber 1.4g | Sugar 22g | Protein 3.3g

Pepper Egg Cups

Prep Time: 15 minutes.
Cook Time: 18 minutes.
Serves: 4

Ingredients:

- 2 bell pepper, halved, seeds removed
- 4 eggs
- 1 teaspoon olive oil
- 1 pinch salt and black pepper
- 1 pinch sriracha flakes

Preparation:

1. Slice the bell peppers in half, lengthwise, and remove their seeds and the inner portion to get a cup-like shape.
2. Rub olive oil on the edges of the bell peppers.
3. Place them in the two Air Fryer Baskets with their cut side up and crack 1 egg in each half of bell pepper.
4. Drizzle salt, black pepper, and sriracha flakes on top of the eggs.
5. Return the Air Fryer Baskets to the Air Fryer.
6. Choose the Air Fryer mode for Zone 1 with 390 degrees F temperature and 18 minutes cooking time.
7. Select the "MATCH COOK" option to copy the settings for Zone 2.
8. Initiate cooking by pressing the START/PAUSE BUTTON.
9. Serve warm and fresh.

Serving Suggestion: Serve the cups with toasted bread slices and crispy bacon.

Variation Tip: Broil the cups with mozzarella cheese on top.

Nutritional Information Per Serving:
Calories 183 | Fat 15g |Sodium 402mg | Carbs 2.5g | Fiber 0.4g | Sugar 1.1g | Protein 10g

Breakfast Bacon

Prep Time: 10 minutes.
Cook Time: 14 minutes.
Serves: 4

Ingredients:

- ½ lb of bacon slices

Preparation:

1. Spread half of the bacon slices in each of the Air Fryer baskets evenly in a single layer.
2. Return the Air Fryer Baskets to the Air Fryer.
3. Choose the Air Fryer mode for Zone 1 with 390 degrees F temperature and 14 minutes cooking time.
4. Select the "MATCH COOK" option to copy the settings for Zone 2.
5. Initiate cooking by pressing the START/PAUSE BUTTON.
6. Flip the crispy bacon once cooked halfway through, then resume cooking.
7. Serve.

Serving Suggestion: Serve the bacon with eggs and bread slices

Variation Tip: Add salt and black pepper for seasoning.

Nutritional Information Per Serving:

Calories 273 | Fat 22g |Sodium 517mg | Carbs 3.3g | Fiber 0.2g | Sugar 1.4g | Protein 16.1g

Biscuit Balls

Prep Time: 10 minutes.
Cook Time: 18 minutes.
Serves: 6

Ingredients:

- 1 tablespoon butter
- 2 eggs, beaten
- ¼ teaspoons pepper
- 1 can (10.2 oz) Pillsbury Buttermilk biscuits
- 2 ounces cheddar cheese, diced into ten cubes
- Cooking spray
- Egg Wash
- 1 egg

- 1 tablespoon water

Preparation:

1. Place a suitable non-stick skillet over medium-high heat and cook the bacon until crispy, then place it on a plate lined with a paper towel.
2. Melt butter in the same skillet over medium heat. Beat eggs with pepper in a bowl and pour them into the skillet.
3. Stir cook for 5 minutes, then remove it from the heat.
4. Add bacon and mix well.
5. Divide the dough into 5 biscuits and slice each into 2 layers.
6. Press each biscuit into 4 inches round.
7. Add a tablespoon of the egg mixture at the center of each round and top it with a piece of cheese.
8. Carefully fold the biscuit dough around the filling and pinch the edges to seal.
9. Whisk egg with water in a small bowl and brush the egg wash over the biscuits.
10. Place half of the biscuit bombs in each of the Air Fryer Baskets and spray them with cooking oil.
11. Return the Air Fryer Baskets to the Air Fryer.
12. Choose the Air Fryer mode for Zone 1 with 375 degrees F temperature and 14 minutes cooking time.
13. Select the "MATCH COOK" option to copy the settings for Zone 2.
14. Initiate cooking by pressing the START/PAUSE BUTTON.
15. Flip the egg bombs when cooked halfway through, then resume cooking.
16. Serve warm

Serving Suggestion: Serve the eggs balls with crispy bacon.

Variation Tip: Add dried herbs to the egg filling.

Nutritional Information Per Serving:

Calories 102 | Fat 7.6g |Sodium 545mg | Carbs 1.5g | Fiber 0.4g | Sugar 0.7g | Protein 7.1g

Morning Egg Rolls

Prep Time: 15 minutes.
Cook Time: 13 minutes.
Serves: 6

Ingredients:

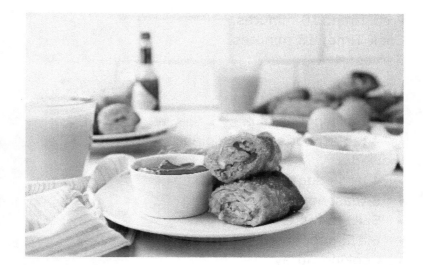

- 2 eggs
- 2 tablespoons milk
- Salt, to taste
- Black pepper, to taste
- 1/2 cup shredded cheddar cheese
- 2 sausage patties
- 6 egg roll wrappers
- 1 tablespoon olive oil
- 1 cup of water

Preparation:

1. Grease a small skillet with some olive oil and place it over medium heat.
2. Add sausage patties and cook them until brown.
3. Chop the cooked patties into small pieces. Beat eggs with salt, black pepper, and milk in a mixing bowl.
4. Grease the same skillet with 1 teaspoon olive oil and pour the egg mixture into it.
5. Stir cook to make scrambled eggs.
6. Add sausage, mix well and remove the skillet from the heat.
7. Spread an egg roll wrapper on the working surface in a diamond shape position.
8. Add a tablespoon of cheese at the bottom third of the roll wrapper.
9. Top the cheese with egg mixture and wet the edges of the wrapper with water.
10. Fold the two corners of the wrapper and roll it, then seal the edges.
11. Repeat the same steps and divide the rolls in the two Air Fryer Baskets.
12. Return the Air Fryer Baskets to the Air Fryer.
13. Choose the Air Fryer mode for Zone 1 with 375 degrees F temperature and 13 minutes cooking time.
14. Select the "MATCH COOK" option to copy the settings for Zone 2.
15. Initiate cooking by pressing the START/PAUSE BUTTON.
16. Flip the rolls after 8 minutes and continue cooking for another 5 minutes.
17. Serve warm and fresh.

Serving Suggestion: Serve the rolls with your favorite hot sauce or cheese dip.

Variation Tip: Add crispy bacon to the filling.

Nutritional Information Per Serving:
Calories 282 | Fat 15g |Sodium 526mg | Carbs 20g | Fiber 0.6g | Sugar 3.3g | Protein 16g

Spinach Egg Muffins

Prep Time: 10 minutes.
Cook Time: 13 minutes.
Serves: 4

Ingredients:

- 4 tablespoons milk
- 4 tablespoons frozen spinach, thawed
- 4 large egg
- 8 teaspoons grated cheese
- Salt, to taste
- Black pepper, to taste
- Cooking Spray

Preparation:

1. Grease four small-sized ramekin with cooking spray.
2. Add egg, cheese, spinach, and milk to a bowl and beat well.
3. Divide the mixture into the four small ramekins and top them with salt and black pepper.
4. Place the two ramekins in each of the two Air Fryer Baskets.
5. Return the Air Fryer Baskets to the Air Fryer.
6. Choose the Air Fryer mode for Zone 1 with 390 degrees F temperature and 13 minutes cooking time.
7. Select the "MATCH COOK" option to copy the settings for Zone 2.
8. Initiate cooking by pressing the START/PAUSE BUTTON.
9. Serve warm.

Serving Suggestion: Serve the muffins with toasted bread slices and crispy bacon.

Variation Tip: Add sliced bell peppers to the muffins.

Nutritional Information Per Serving:

Calories 237 | Fat 19g |Sodium 518mg | Carbs 7g | Fiber 1.5g | Sugar 3.4g | Protein 12g

Pumpkin Muffins

Prep Time: 15 minutes.
Cook Time: 13 minutes.
Serves: 8

Ingredients:

- ½ cup pumpkin puree
- 1 cup gluten-free oats
- ¼ cup honey
- 1 medium egg beaten
- ½ teaspoon coconut butter
- ½ tablespoons cocoa nib
- ½ tablespoons vanilla essence
- Cooking spray
- ½ teaspoon nutmeg

Preparation:

1. Add oats, honey, eggs, pumpkin puree, coconut butter, cocoa nibs, vanilla essence, and nutmeg to a bowl and mix well until smooth.
2. Divide the batter into two 4-cups muffin trays, greased with cooking spray.
3. Place one mini muffin tray in each of the two Air Fryer Baskets.
4. Return the Air Fryer Baskets to the Air Fryer.
5. Choose the Air Fryer mode for Zone 1 with 375 degrees F temperature and 13 minutes cooking time.
6. Select the "MATCH COOK" option to copy the settings for Zone 2.
7. Initiate cooking by pressing the START/PAUSE BUTTON.
8. Allow the muffins to cool, then serve.

Serving Suggestion: Serve the muffins with a hot coffee.

Variation Tip: Add raisins and nuts to the batter before baking.

Nutritional Information Per Serving:

Calories 209 | Fat 7.5g | Sodium 321mg | Carbs 34.1g | Fiber 4g | Sugar 3.8g | Protein 4.3g

Cinnamon Toasts

Prep Time: 15 minutes.
Cook Time: 8 minutes.
Serves: 4

Ingredients:

- 4 pieces of bread
- 2 tablespoons butter
- 2 eggs, beaten
- 1 pinch salt
- 1 pinch cinnamon ground
- 1 pinch nutmeg ground
- 1 pinch ground clove
- 1 teaspoon icing sugar

Preparation:

1. Add two eggs to a mixing bowl and stir cinnamon, nutmeg, ground cloves, and salt, then whisk well.
2. Spread butter on both sides of the bread slices and cut them into thick strips.
3. Dip the breadsticks in the egg mixture and place them in the two Air Fryer baskets.
4. Return the Air Fryer Baskets to the Air Fryer.
5. Choose the Air Fryer mode for Zone 1 with 390 degrees F temperature and 8 minutes cooking time.
6. Select the "MATCH COOK" option to copy the settings for Zone 2.
7. Initiate cooking by pressing the START/PAUSE BUTTON.
8. Flip the French toast sticks when cooked halfway through.
9. Serve.

Serving Suggestion: Serve the toasted with chocolate syrup or Nutella spread.

Variation Tip: Use crushed cornflakes for breading to have extra crispiness.

Nutritional Information Per Serving:

Calories 199 | Fat 11.1g |Sodium 297mg | Carbs 14.9g | Fiber 1g | Sugar 2.5g | Protein 9.9g

Snacks and Appetizers Recipes

Chicken Crescent Wraps

Prep Time: 10 minutes.
Cook Time: 12 minutes.
Serves: 6

Ingredients:

- 3 tablespoons chopped onion
- 3 garlic cloves, peeled and minced
- 3/4 (8 ounces) package cream cheese
- 6 tablespoons butter
- 2 boneless chicken breasts, cubed, cooked
- 3 (10 ounces) cans refrigerated crescent roll dough

Preparation:

1. Heat oil in a skillet and add onion and garlic to sauté until soft.
2. Add cooked chicken, sautéed veggies, butter, and cream cheese to a blender.
3. Blend well until smooth. Spread the crescent dough over a flat surface.
4. Slice the dough into 12 rectangles.
5. Spoon the chicken mixture at the center of each rectangle.
6. Roll the dough to wrap the mixture and form a ball.
7. Divide these balls into the two Air Fryer baskets.
8. Return the Air Fryer Baskets to the Air Fryer.
9. Choose the Air Fryer mode for Zone 1 with 390 degrees F temperature and 12 minutes cooking time.
10. Select the "MATCH COOK" option to copy the settings for Zone 2.
11. Initiate cooking by pressing the START/PAUSE BUTTON.
12. Serve warm

Serving Suggestion: Serve with tomato sauce or cream cheese dip.

Variation Tip: You can also prepare the filling using leftover turkey or pork.

Nutritional Information Per Serving:
Calories 100 | Fat 2g |Sodium 480mg | Carbs 4g | Fiber 2g | Sugar 0g | Protein 18g

Chicken Stuffed Mushrooms

Prep Time: 15 minutes.
Cook Time: 15 minutes.
Serves: 6

Ingredients:

- 6 large fresh mushrooms, stems removed
- Stuffing:
- ½ cup chicken meat, cubed
- 1 (4 ounces) package cream cheese, softened
- ¼ lb. imitation crabmeat, flaked
- 1 cup butter
- 1 garlic clove, peeled and minced
- Black pepper and salt to taste
- Garlic powder to taste
- Crushed red pepper to taste

Preparation:

1. Melt and heat butter in a skillet over medium heat.
2. Add chicken and sauté for 5 minutes.
3. Add in all the remaining ingredients for the stuffing.
4. Cook for 5 minutes, then turn off the heat.
5. Allow the mixture to cool. Stuff each mushroom with a tablespoon of this mixture.
6. Divide the stuffed mushrooms in the two Air Fryer baskets.
7. Return the Air Fryer Baskets to the Air Fryer.
8. Choose the Air Fryer mode for Zone 1 with 375 degrees F temperature and 15 minutes cooking time.
9. Select the "MATCH COOK" option to copy the settings for Zone 2.
10. Initiate cooking by pressing the START/PAUSE BUTTON.
11. Serve warm.

Serving Suggestion: Serve with mayonnaise or cream cheese dip.

Variation Tip: Use crushed cornflakes for breading to have extra crispiness.

Nutritional Information Per Serving:
Calories 180 | Fat 3.2g |Sodium 133mg | Carbs 32g | Fiber 1.1g | Sugar 1.8g | Protein 9g

Onion Rings

Prep Time: 10 minutes.
Cook Time: 22 minutes.
Serves: 4

Ingredients:

- ¾ cup all-purpose flour
- 1 teaspoon salt
- 1 large onion, cut into rings
- ½ cup cornstarch
- 2 teaspoons baking powder
- 1 cup low-fat milk
- 1 egg
- 1 cup bread crumbs
- 1/6 teaspoons paprika
- Cooking spray
- 1/6 teaspoons garlic powder

Preparation:

1. Mix flour with baking powder, cornstarch, and salt in a small bowl.
2. First, coat the onion rings with flour mixture; set them aside.
3. Beat milk with egg, then add the remaining flour mixture into the egg.
4. Mix them well together to make a thick batter.
5. Now dip the floured onion rings into the prepared batter and coat them well.
6. Place the rings on a wire rack for 10 minutes.
7. Spread bread crumbs in a shallow bowl.
8. Coat the onion rings with breadcrumbs and shake off the excess.
9. Set the coated onion rings in the two Air fryer baskets.
10. Spray all the rings with the cooking spray.
11. Return the Air Fryer Baskets to the Air Fryer.
12. Choose the Air Fryer mode for Zone 1 with 375 degrees F temperature and 22 minutes cooking time.
13. Select the "MATCH COOK" option to copy the settings for Zone 2.
14. Initiate cooking by pressing the START/PAUSE BUTTON.
15. Flip once cooked halfway through, then resume cooking
16. Season the air fried onion rings with garlic powder and paprika.
17. Serve.

Serving Suggestion: Serve with tomato sauce or cream cheese dip.

Variation Tip: Use crushed cornflakes for breading to have extra crispiness.

Nutritional Information Per Serving:

Calories 229 | Fat 1.9 |Sodium 567mg | Carbs 1.9g | Fiber 0.4g | Sugar 0.6g | Protein 11.8g

Potato Tater Tots

Prep Time: 10 minutes.
Cook Time: 27 minutes.
Serves: 4

Ingredients:

- 2 potatoes, peeled
- 1/2 teaspoons Cajun seasoning
- Olive oil cooking spray
- Sea salt to taste

Preparation:

1. Boil water in a cooking pot and cook potatoes in it for 15 minutes.
2. Drain and leave the potatoes to cool in a bowl.
3. Grate these potatoes and toss them with Cajun seasoning.
4. Make small tater tots out of this mixture.
5. Divide them into the two Air Fryer baskets and spray them with cooking oil.
6. Return the Air Fryer Baskets to the Air Fryer.
7. Choose the Air Fryer mode for Zone 1 with 375 degrees F temperature and 27 minutes cooking time.

8. Select the "MATCH COOK" option to copy the settings for Zone 2.
9. Initiate cooking by pressing the START/PAUSE BUTTON.
10. Flip them once cooked halfway through, and resume cooking.
11. Serve warm

Serving Suggestion: Serve with ketchup, mayonnaise, or cream cheese dip.

Variation Tip: Use crushed cornflakes for breading to have extra crispiness.

Nutritional Information Per Serving:

Calories 185 | Fat 11g |Sodium 355mg | Carbs 21g | Fiber 5.8g | Sugar 3g | Protein 4.7g

Crispy Plantain Chips

Prep Time: 15 minutes.
Cook Time: 20 minutes.
Serves: 4

Ingredients:

- 1 green plantain
- 1 teaspoon canola oil
- 1/2 teaspoons sea salt

Preparation:

1. Peel and cut the plantains into long strips using a mandolin slicer.
2. Grease the Air Fryer basket with a ½ teaspoon with canola oil.
3. Toss the plantains with salt and remaining canola oil.
4. Divide these plantains in the two Air fryer baskets.
5. Return the Air Fryer Baskets to the Air Fryer.
6. Choose the Air Fryer mode for Zone 1 with 350 degrees F temperature and 20 minutes cooking time.
7. Select the "MATCH COOK" option to copy the settings for Zone 2.
8. Initiate cooking by pressing the START/PAUSE BUTTON.
9. Toss the plantains after 10 minutes and resume cooking.
10. Serve warm.

Serving Suggestion: Serve with cream cheese dip and celery sticks.

Variation Tip: Use black pepper to season the chips.

Nutritional Information Per Serving:

Calories 122 | Fat 1.8g |Sodium 794mg | Carbs 17g | Fiber 8.9g | Sugar 1.6g | Protein 14.9g

Peppered Asparagus

Prep Time: 10 minutes.
Cook Time: 16 minutes.
Serves: 6

Ingredients:

- 1 bunch of asparagus, trimmed
- Avocado or Olive Oil
- Himalayan salt, to taste
- Black pepper, to taste

Preparation:

1. Divide the asparagus in the two Air Fryer baskets.
2. Toss the asparagus with salt, black pepper, and oil.
3. Return the Air Fryer Baskets to the Air Fryer.
4. Choose the Air Fryer mode for Zone 1 with 390 degrees F temperature and 16 minutes cooking time.
5. Select the "MATCH COOK" option to copy the settings for Zone 2.
6. Initiate cooking by pressing the START/PAUSE BUTTON.
7. Serve warm.

Serving Suggestion: Serve with mayonnaise or cream cheese dip.

Variation Tip: Use panko crumbs for breading to have extra crispiness.

Nutritional Information Per Serving:
Calories 163 | Fat 11.5g |Sodium 918mg | Carbs 8.3g | Fiber 4.2g | Sugar 0.2g | Protein 7.4g

Cauliflower Gnocchi

Prep Time: 15 minutes.
Cook Time: 17 minutes.
Serves: 5

Ingredients:

- 1 bag frozen cauliflower gnocchi
- 1 ½ tablespoon olive oil
- 1 teaspoon garlic powder
- 3 tablespoons parmesan, grated
- 1/2 teaspoons dried basil
- Salt to taste
- Fresh chopped parsley for topping

Preparation:

1. Toss gnocchi with olive oil, garlic powder, 1 tbsp parmesan, salt, and basil in a bowl.
2. Divide the gnocchi in the two air fryer baskets.
3. Return the Air Fryer Baskets to the Air Fryer.
4. Choose the Air Fryer mode for Zone 1 with 400 degrees F temperature and 10 minutes cooking time.
5. Select the "MATCH COOK" option to copy the settings for Zone 2.
6. Initiate cooking by pressing the START/PAUSE BUTTON.
7. Toss the gnocchi once cooked halfway through, then resume cooking.
8. Drizzle the remaining parmesan on top of the gnocchi and cook again for 7 minutes.
9. Serve warm.

Serving Suggestion: Serve with tomato or sweet chili sauce.

Variation Tip: Use crushed cornflakes for breading to have extra crispiness.

Nutritional Information Per Serving:

Calories 134 | Fat 5.9g |Sodium 343mg | Carbs 9.5g | Fiber 0.5g | Sugar 1.1g | Protein 10.4g

Fried Halloumi Cheese

Prep Time: 10 minutes.
Cook Time: 12 minutes.
Serves: 6

Ingredients:

*   1 block of halloumi cheese, sliced
*   2 teaspoons olive oil

Preparation:

1. Divide the halloumi cheese slices in the air fryer baskets.
2. Drizzle olive oil over the cheese slices.
3. Return the Air Fryer Baskets to the Air Fryer.
4. Choose the Air Fryer mode for Zone 1 with 360 degrees F temperature and 12 minutes cooking time.
5. Flip the cheese slices once cooked halfway through.
6. Serve.

Serving Suggestion: Serve with fresh yogurt dip or cucumber salad.

Variation Tip: Add black pepper and salt for seasoning.

Nutritional Information Per Serving:

Calories 186 | Fat 3g |Sodium 223mg | Carbs 31g | Fiber 8.7g | Sugar 5.5g | Protein 9.7g

Crispy Tortilla Chips

Prep Time: 15 minutes.
Cook Time: 13 minutes.
Serves: 8

Ingredients:

- 4 (6-inch) corn tortillas
- 1 tablespoon Avocado Oil
- Sea salt to taste
- Cooking spray

Preparation:

1. Spread the corn tortillas on the working surface.
2. Slice them into bite-sized triangles.
3. Toss them with salt and cooking oil.
4. Divide the triangles in the two Air fryer baskets into a single layer.
5. Return the Air Fryer Baskets to the Air Fryer.
6. Choose the Air Fryer mode for Zone 1 with 390 degrees F temperature and 13 minutes cooking time.
7. Select the "MATCH COOK" option to copy the settings for Zone 2.
8. Initiate cooking by pressing the START/PAUSE BUTTON.
9. Toss the chips once cooked halfway through, then resume cooking.
10. Serve and enjoy.

Serving Suggestion: Serve with guacamole, mayonnaise, or cream cheese dip.

Variation Tip: Drizzle parmesan cheese on top before Air Frying.

Nutritional Information Per Serving:
Calories 103 | Fat 8.4g |Sodium 117mg | Carbs 3.5g | Fiber 0.9g | Sugar 1.5g | Protein 5.1g

Parmesan French Fries

Prep Time: 10 minutes.
Cook Time: 20 minutes.
Serves: 6

Ingredients:

- 3 medium russet potatoes
- 2 tablespoons parmesan cheese
- 2 tablespoons fresh parsley, chopped
- 1 tablespoon olive oil
- Salt, to taste

Preparation:

1. Wash the potatoes and pass them through the fries' cutter to get ¼ inch thick fries.
2. Place the fries in a colander and drizzle salt on top.
3. Leave these fries for 10 minutes, then rinse.
4. Toss the potatoes with parmesan cheese, oil, salt, and parsley in a bowl.
5. Divide the potatoes into the two air fryer baskets.
6. Return the Air Fryer Baskets to the Air Fryer.
7. Choose the Air Fryer mode for Zone 1 with 360 degrees F temperature and 20 minutes cooking time.
8. Select the "MATCH COOK" option to copy the settings for Zone 2.
9. Initiate cooking by pressing the START/PAUSE BUTTON.
10. Toss the chips once cooked halfway through, then resume cooking.
11. Serve warm.

Serving Suggestion: Serve with tomato ketchup, Asian coleslaw, or creamed cabbage.

Variation Tip: Toss fries with black pepper for change of taste.

Nutritional Information Per Serving:

Calories 307 | Fat 8.6g |Sodium 510mg | Carbs 22.2g | Fiber 1.4g | Sugar 13g | Protein 33.6g

Vegetables and Sides Recipes

Lime Glazed Tofu

Prep Time: 10 minutes.
Cook Time: 14 minutes.
Serves: 6

Ingredients:

* ⅔ cup coconut aminos
* 2 (14 oz) packages extra-firm, water-packed tofu, drained
* 6 tablespoons toasted sesame oil
* ⅔ cup lime juice

Preparation:

1. Pat dry the tofu bars and slice into half-inch cubes.
2. Toss all the remaining ingredients in a small bowl.
3. Marinate for 4 hours in the refrigerator. Drain off the excess water.
4. Divide the tofu cubes in the two Air Fryer baskets.
5. Return the Air Fryer Baskets to the Air Fryer.
6. Choose the Air Fryer mode for Zone 1 with 400 degrees F temperature and 14 minutes cooking time.
7. Select the "MATCH COOK" option to copy the settings for Zone 2.
8. Initiate cooking by pressing the START/PAUSE BUTTON.
9. Toss the tofu once cooked halfway through, then resume cooking.
10. Serve warm

Serving Suggestion: Serve with sautéed green vegetables.

Variation Tip: Add sautéed onion and carrot to the tofu cubes.

Nutritional Information Per Serving:

Calories 284 | Fat 7.9g |Sodium 704mg | Carbs 38.1g | Fiber 1.9g | Sugar 1.9g | Protein 14.8g

Falafel

Prep Time: 15 minutes.
Cook Time: 14 minutes.
Serves: 6

Ingredients:

- 1 (15.5 oz) can chickpeas, rinsed and drained
- 1 small yellow onion, cut into quarters
- 3 garlic cloves, chopped
- 1/3 cup parsley, chopped
- 1/3 cup cilantro, chopped
- 1/3 cup scallions, chopped
- 1 teaspoon cumin
- 1/2 teaspoons salt
- 1/8 teaspoons crushed red pepper flakes

- 1 teaspoon baking powder
- 4 tablespoons all-purpose flour
- Olive oil spray

Preparation:

1. Dry the chickpeas on paper towels.
2. Add onions and garlic to a food processor and chop them.
3. Add the parsley, salt, cilantro, scallions, cumin, and red pepper flakes.
4. Press the pulse button for 60 seconds, then toss in chickpeas and blend for 3 times until it makes a chunky paste.
5. Stir in baking powder and flour and mix well.
6. Transfer the falafel mixture to a bowl and cover to refrigerate for 3 hours.
7. Make 12 balls out of the falafel mixture.
8. Place 6 falafels in each of the Air Fryer baskets and spray them with oil.
9. Return the Air Fryer Baskets to the Air Fryer.
10. Choose the Air Fryer mode for Zone 1 with 350 degrees F temperature and 14 minutes cooking time.
11. Select the "MATCH COOK" option to copy the settings for Zone 2.
12. Initiate cooking by pressing the START/PAUSE BUTTON.
13. Toss the falafel once cooked halfway through, and resume cooking.
14. Serve warm

Serving Suggestion: Serve with yogurt dip and sautéed carrots.

Variation Tip: Use breadcrumbs for breading to have extra crispiness.

Nutritional Information Per Serving:
Calories 113 | Fat 3g |Sodium 152mg | Carbs 20g | Fiber 3g | Sugar 1.1g | Protein 3.5g

Saucy Carrots

Prep Time: 15 minutes.
Cook Time: 25 minutes.
Serves: 6

Ingredients:

- 1 lb. cup carrots, cut into chunks
- 1 tablespoon sesame oil
- ½ tablespoons ginger, minced
- ½ tablespoons soy sauce
- ½ teaspoon garlic, minced
- ½ tablespoons scallions, chopped, for garnish
- ½ teaspoon sesame seeds for garnish

Preparation:

1. Toss all the ginger carrots ingredients, except the sesame seeds and scallions, in a suitable bowl.
2. Divide the carrots in the two Air Fryer Baskets in a single layer.
3. Return the Air Fryer Baskets to the Air Fryer.
4. Choose the Air Fryer mode for Zone 1 with 390 degrees F temperature and 25 minutes cooking time.
5. Select the "MATCH COOK" option to copy the settings for Zone 2.
6. Initiate cooking by pressing the START/PAUSE BUTTON.
7. Toss the carrots once cooked halfway through.
8. Garnish with sesame seeds and scallions.
9. Serve warm

Serving Suggestion: Serve with mayo sauce or ketchup.

Variation Tip: Use some honey for a sweet taste.

Nutritional Information Per Serving:

Calories 206 | Fat 3.4g |Sodium 174mg | Carbs 35g | Fiber 9.4g | Sugar 5.9g | Protein 10.6g

Zucchini Cakes

Prep Time: 10 minutes.
Cook Time: 32 minutes.
Serves: 6

Ingredients:

- 2 medium zucchinis, grated
- 1 cup corn kernel
- 1 medium potato cooked
- 2 tablespoons chickpea flour
- 2 garlic minced
- 2 teaspoons olive oil
- Salt and black pepper
- For Serving:
- Yogurt tahini sauce

Preparation:

1. Mix grated zucchini with a pinch of salt in a colander and leave them for 15 minutes.
2. Squeeze out their excess water.
3. Mash the cooked potato in a large-sized bowl with a fork.
4. Add zucchini, corn, garlic, chickpea flour, salt, and black pepper to the bowl.
5. Mix these fritters' ingredients together and make 2 tablespoons-sized balls out of this mixture and flatten them lightly.
6. Divide the fritters in the two Air Fryer baskets in a single layer and spray them with cooking.
7. Return the Air Fryer Baskets to the Air Fryer.
8. Choose the Air Fryer mode for Zone 1 with 390 degrees F temperature and 17 minutes cooking time.
9. Select the "MATCH COOK" option to copy the settings for Zone 2.
10. Initiate cooking by pressing the START/PAUSE BUTTON.
11. Flip the fritters once cooked halfway through, then resume cooking.
12. Serve

Serving Suggestion: Serve with mayonnaise or cream cheese dip.

Variation Tip: Use crushed cornflakes for breading to have extra crispiness.

Nutritional Information Per Serving:
Calories 270 | Fat 14.6g |Sodium 394mg | Carbs 31.3g | Fiber 7.5g | Sugar 9.7g | Protein 6.4g

Quinoa Patties

Prep Time: 15 minutes.
Cook Time: 32 minutes.
Serves: 4

Ingredients:

- 1 cup quinoa red
- 1½ cups water
- 1 teaspoon salt
- black pepper, ground
- 1½ cups rolled oats
- 3 eggs beaten
- ¼ cup minced white onion
- ½ cup crumbled feta cheese
- ¼ cup chopped fresh chives
- Salt and black pepper, to taste
- Vegetable or canola oil
- 4 hamburger buns
- 4 arugulas
- 4 slices tomato sliced

Cucumber yogurt dill sauce
- 1 cup cucumber, diced
- 1 cup Greek yogurt
- 2 teaspoons lemon juice
- ¼ teaspoons salt
- Black pepper, ground
- 1 tablespoon chopped fresh dill
- 1 tablespoon olive oil

Preparation:

1. Add quinoa to a saucepan filled with cold water, salt, and black pepper, and place it over medium-high heat.
2. Cook the quinoa to a boil, then reduce the heat, cover, and cook for 20 minutes on a simmer.
3. Fluff and mix the cooked quinoa with a fork and remove it from the heat.
4. Spread the quinoa in a baking stay.
5. Mix eggs, oats, onion, herbs, cheese, salt, and black pepper.
6. Stir in quinoa, then mix well. Make 4 patties out of this quinoa cheese mixture.
7. Divide the patties in the two Air Fryer Baskets and spray them with cooking oil.
8. Return the Air Fryer Baskets to the Air Fryer.

9. Choose the Air Fryer mode for Zone 1 with 390 degrees F temperature and 13 minutes cooking time.
10. Select the "MATCH COOK" option to copy the settings for Zone 2.
11. Initiate cooking by pressing the START/PAUSE BUTTON.
12. Flip the patties once cooked halfway through, and resume cooking.
13. Meanwhile, prepare the cucumber yogurt dill sauce by mixing all of its ingredients in a mixing bowl.
14. Place each quinoa patty in a burger bun along with arugula leaves.
15. Serve with yogurt dill sauce.

Serving Suggestion: Serve with yogurt dip.

Variation Tip: Use crushed cornflakes for breading to have extra crispiness.

Nutritional Information Per Serving:
Calories 231 | Fat 9g |Sodium 271mg | Carbs 32.8g | Fiber 6.4g | Sugar 7g | Protein 6.3g

Air Fried Okra

Prep Time: 10 minutes.
Cook Time: 13 minutes.
Serves: 2

Ingredients:

- ½ lb okra pods sliced
- 1 teaspoon olive oil
- ¼ teaspoons salt
- ⅛ teaspoons black pepper

Preparation:

1. Preheat your Air Fryer Machine to 350 F.
2. Toss okra with olive oil, salt, and black pepper in a bowl.
3. Spread the okra in a single layer in the two Air Fryer Baskets.
4. Return the Air Fryer Baskets to the Air Fryer.
5. Choose the Air Fryer mode for Zone 1 with 375 degrees F temperature and 13 minutes cooking time.
6. Select the "MATCH COOK" option to copy the settings for Zone 2.
7. Initiate cooking by pressing the START/PAUSE BUTTON.
8. Toss the okra once cooked halfway through, and resume cooking.
9. Serve warm

Serving Suggestion: Serve with potato chips and bread slices.

Variation Tip: Sprinkle cornmeal before cooking for added crisp.

Nutritional Information Per Serving:
Calories 208 | Fat 5g |Sodium 1205mg | Carbs 34.1g | Fiber 7.8g | Sugar 2.5g | Protein 5.9g

Hasselback Potatoes

Prep Time: 15 minutes.
Cook Time: 15 minutes.
Serves: 4

Ingredients:

- 4 medium Yukon Gold potatoes
- 3 tablespoons melted butter
- 1 tablespoon olive oil
- 3 garlic cloves, crushed
- ½ teaspoon ground paprika
- Salt and black pepper ground, to taste
- 1 tablespoon chopped fresh parsley

Preparation:

1. Slice each potato from the top to make 1/4-inch slices without cutting its 1/2-inch bottom, keeping the potato's bottom intact.
2. Mix butter with olive oil, garlic, and paprika in a small bowl.
3. Brush the garlic mixture on top of each potato and add the mixture into the slits.
4. Season them with salt and black pepper.
5. Place 2 seasoned potatoes in each of the Air Fryer Baskets
6. Return the Air Fryer Baskets to the Air Fryer.
7. Choose the Air Fryer mode for Zone 1 with 375 degrees F temperature and 25 minutes cooking time.
8. Select the "MATCH COOK" option to copy the settings for Zone 2.
9. Initiate cooking by pressing the START/PAUSE BUTTON.
10. Brushing the potatoes again with butter mixture after 15 minutes, then resume cooking.
11. Garnish with parsley.
12. Serve warm

Serving Suggestion: Serve with mayonnaise or cream cheese dip.

Variation Tip: Add tomato and cheese slices to the potato slits before air frying.

Nutritional Information Per Serving:
Calories 350 | Fat 2.6g |Sodium 358mg | Carbs 64.6g | Fiber 14.4g | Sugar 3.3g | Protein 19.9g

Fried Olives

Prep Time: 15 minutes.
Cook Time: 9 minutes.
Serves: 6

Ingredients:

- 2 cups blue cheese stuffed olives, drained
- 1/2 cup all-purpose flour
- 1 cup panko breadcrumbs
- 1/2 teaspoons garlic powder
- 1 pinch of oregano
- 2 eggs

Preparation:

1. Mix flour with oregano and garlic powder in a bowl and beat two eggs in another bowl.
2. Spread panko breadcrumbs in a bowl.
3. Coat all the olives with the flour mixture, dip in the eggs and then coat with the panko breadcrumbs.
4. As you coat the olives, place them in the two air fryer baskets in a single layer, then spray them with cooking oil.
5. Return the Air Fryer Baskets to the Air Fryer.
6. Choose the Air Fryer mode for Zone 1 with 375 degrees F temperature and 9 minutes cooking time.
7. Select the "MATCH COOK" option to copy the settings for Zone 2.
8. Initiate cooking by pressing the START/PAUSE BUTTON.
9. Flip the olives once cooked halfway through, then resume cooking.
10. Serve.

Serving Suggestion: Serve with red chunky salsa or chili sauce.

Variation Tip: Use crushed cornflakes for breading to have extra crispiness.

Nutritional Information Per Serving:

Calories 166 | Fat 3.2g |Sodium 437mg | Carbs 28.8g | Fiber 1.8g | Sugar 2.7g | Protein 5.8g

Fried Artichoke Hearts

Prep Time: 15 minutes.
Cook Time: 10 minutes.
Serves: 6

Ingredients:

- 3 cans Quartered Artichokes, drained
- 1/2 cup mayonnaise
- 1 cup panko breadcrumbs
- ⅓ cup grated Parmesan
- salt and black pepper to taste
- Parsley for garnish

Preparation:

1. Mix mayonnaise with salt and black pepper and keep the sauce aside.
2. Spread panko breadcrumbs in a bowl.
3. Coat the artichoke pieces with the breadcrumbs.
4. As you coat the artichokes, place them in the two air fryer baskets in a single layer, then spray them with cooking oil.
5. Return the Air Fryer Baskets to the Air Fryer.
6. Choose the Air Fryer mode for Zone 1 with 375 degrees F temperature and 10 minutes cooking time.
7. Select the "MATCH COOK" option to copy the settings for Zone 2.
8. Initiate cooking by pressing the START/PAUSE BUTTON.
9. Flip the artichokes once cooked halfway through, then resume cooking.
10. Serve warm with mayo sauce.

Serving Suggestion: Serve with red chunky salsa or chili sauce.

Variation Tip: Use crushed cornflakes for breading to have extra crispiness.

Nutritional Information Per Serving:

Calories 193 | Fat 1g | Sodium 395mg | Carbs 38.7g | Fiber 1.6g | Sugar 0.9g | Protein 6.6g

Sweet Potatoes with Honey Butter

Prep Time: 15 minutes.
Cook Time: 40 minutes.
Serves: 4

Ingredients:

- 4 sweet potatoes, scrubbed
- 1 teaspoon oil

Honey Butter

- 4 tablespoons unsalted butter
- 1 tablespoon Honey
- 2 teaspoons hot sauce
- ¼ teaspoons salt

Preparation:

1. Rub the sweet potatoes with oil and place two potatoes in each air fryer basket.
2. Return the Air Fryer Baskets to the Air Fryer.
3. Choose the Air Fryer mode for Zone 1 with 400 degrees F temperature and 40 minutes cooking time.
4. Select the "MATCH COOK" option to copy the settings for Zone 2.
5. Initiate cooking by pressing the START/PAUSE BUTTON.
6. Flip the potatoes once cooked halfway through, then resume cooking.
7. Mix butter with hot sauce, honey, and salt in a bowl.
8. When the potatoes are done, cut a slit on top and make a well with a spoon
9. Pour the honey butter in each potato jacket.
10. Serve.

Serving Suggestion: Serve with sautéed vegetables and salad.

Variation Tip: Sprinkle crumbled bacon and parsley on top.

Nutritional Information Per Serving:

Calories 288 | Fat 6.9g |Sodium 761mg | Carbs 46g | Fiber 4g | Sugar 12g | Protein 9.6g

Curly Fries

Prep Time: 10 minutes.
Cook Time: 20 minutes.
Serves: 6

Ingredients:

- 2 Spiralized Zucchinis
- 1 cup flour
- 2 tbs paprika
- 1 teaspoon cayenne pepper
- 1 teaspoon garlic powder
- 1 teaspoon black pepper
- 1 teaspoon salt
- 2 eggs
- olive oil or cooking spray

Preparation:

1. Mix flour with paprika, cayenne pepper, garlic powder, black pepper, and salt in a bowl.
2. Beat eggs in another bowl and dip the zucchini in the eggs.
3. Coat the zucchini with the flour mixture and divide it into two air fryer baskets.
4. Spray the zucchini with cooking oil.
5. Return the Air Fryer Baskets to the Air Fryer.
6. Choose the Air Fryer mode for Zone 1 with 400 degrees F temperature and 20 minutes cooking time.
7. Select the "MATCH COOK" option to copy the settings for Zone 2.
8. Initiate cooking by pressing the START/PAUSE BUTTON.
9. Toss the zucchini once cooked halfway through, then resume cooking.
10. Serve warm.

Serving Suggestion: Serve with red chunky salsa or chili sauce.

Variation Tip: Use crushed cornflakes for breading to have extra crispiness.

Nutritional Information Per Serving:

Calories 212 | Fat 11.8g |Sodium 321mg | Carbs 24.6g | Fiber 4.4g | Sugar 8g | Protein 7.3g

Fish and Seafood Recipes

Salmon Patties

Prep Time: 15 minutes.
Cook Time: 18 minutes.
Serves: 8
Ingredients:
*   1 lb fresh Atlantic salmon side
*   1/4 cup avocado, mashed
*   1/4 cup cilantro, diced
*   1 1/2 teaspoons yellow curry powder
*   1/2 teaspoons sea salt
*   1/4 cup, 4 teaspoons tapioca starch
*   2 brown eggs
*   1/2 cup coconut flakes
*   Coconut oil, melted, for brushing
*   For the greens:
*   2 teaspoons organic coconut oil, melted

*   6 cups arugula & spinach mix, tightly packed
*   Pinch of sea salt

Preparation:
1. Remove the fish skin and dice the flesh.
2. Place in a large bowl. Add cilantro, avocado, salt, and curry powder mix gently.
3. Add tapioca starch and mix well again.
4. Make 8 salmon patties out of this mixture, about a half-inch thick.
5. Place them on a baking sheet lined with wax paper and freeze them for 20 minutes.
6. Place ¼ cup tapioca starch and coconut flakes on a flat plate.
7. Dip the patties in the whisked egg, then coat the frozen patties in the starch and flakes.
8. Place half of the patties in each of the Air Fryer Baskets and spray them with cooking oil
9. Return the Air Fryer Baskets to the Air Fryer.
10. Choose the Air Fryer mode for Zone 1 with 390 degrees F temperature and 17 minutes cooking time.
11. Select the "MATCH COOK" option to copy the settings for Zone 2.
12. Initiate cooking by pressing the START/PAUSE BUTTON.
13. Flip the patties once cooked halfway through, then resume cooking.
14. Sauté arugula with spinach in coconut oil in a pan for 30 seconds.
15. Serve the patties with sautéed greens mixture
Serving Suggestion: Serve with sautéed green beans or asparagus.
Variation Tip: Add lemon juice to the mixture before mixing.
Nutritional Information Per Serving:
Calories 260 | Fat 16g |Sodium 585mg | Carbs 3.1g | Fiber 1.3g | Sugar 0.2g | Protein 25.5g

Scallops with Greens

Prep Time: 15 minutes.
Cook Time: 13 minutes.
Serves: 8

Ingredients:

- 3/4 cup heavy whipping cream
- 1 tablespoon tomato paste
- 1 tablespoon chopped fresh basil
- 1 teaspoon garlic, minced
- 1/2 teaspoons salt
- 1/2 teaspoons pepper
- 12 ounces frozen spinach thawed
- 8 jumbo sea scallops
- Vegetable oil to spray

Preparation:

1. Season the scallops with vegetable oil, salt, and pepper in a bowl
2. Mix cream with spinach, basil, garlic, salt, pepper, and tomato paste in a bowl.
3. Pour this mixture over the scallops and mix gently.
4. Divide the scallops in the Air Fryers Baskets without using the crisper plate.
5. Return the Air Fryer Baskets to the Air Fryer.
6. Choose the Air Fryer mode for Zone 1 with 390 degrees F temperature and 13 minutes cooking time.
7. Select the "MATCH COOK" option to copy the settings for Zone 2.
8. Initiate cooking by pressing the START/PAUSE BUTTON.
9. Serve right away

Serving Suggestion: Serve with fresh cucumber salad.

Variation Tip: Use crushed cornflakes for breading to have extra crispiness.

Nutritional Information Per Serving:
Calories 266 | Fat 6.3g |Sodium 193mg | Carbs 39.1g | Fiber 7.2g | Sugar 5.2g | Protein 14.8g

Crusted Shrimp

Prep Time: 20 minutes.
Cook Time: 13 minutes.
Serves: 4

Ingredients:

- 1 lb shrimp
- 1/2 cup flour, all-purpose
- 1 teaspoon salt
- 1/2 teaspoons baking powder
- 2/3 cup water
- 2 cups coconut shred
- 1/2 cup bread crumbs

Preparation:

1. In a small bowl, whisk together flour, salt, water, and baking powder. Set aside for 5 minutes.
2. In another shallow bowl, toss bread crumbs with coconut shreds together.
3. Dredge shrimp in liquid, then coat in coconut mixture, making sure it's totally covered.
4. Repeat until all shrimp are coated.
5. Spread half of the shrimp in each air fryer basket and spray them with cooking oil.
6. Return the Air Fryer Baskets to the Air Fryer.
7. Choose the Air Fryer mode for Zone 1 with 390 degrees F temperature and 13 minutes cooking time.
8. Select the "MATCH COOK" option to copy the settings for Zone 2.
9. Initiate cooking by pressing the START/PAUSE BUTTON.
10. Shake the baskets once cooked halfway, then resume cooking.
11. Serve with your favorite dip.

Serving Suggestion: Serve on top of mashed potato or mashed cauliflower.

Variation Tip: Use crushed cornflakes for breading to have extra crispiness.

Nutritional Information Per Serving:
Calories 297 | Fat 1g |Sodium 291mg | Carbs 35g | Fiber 1g | Sugar 9g | Protein 29g

Fish Sandwich

Prep Time: 15 minutes.
Cook Time: 22 minutes.
Serves: 4

Ingredients:

- 4 small cod fillets, skinless
- Salt and black pepper, to taste
- 2 tablespoons flour
- ¼ cup dried breadcrumbs
- Spray oil
- 9 ounces of frozen peas
- 1 tablespoon creme fraiche
- 12 capers
- 1 squeeze of lemon juice
- 4 bread rolls, cut in halve

Preparation:

1. First, coat the cod fillets with flour, salt, and black pepper.
2. Then coat the fish with breadcrumbs.
3. Divide the coated codfish in the two Air fryer baskets and spray them with cooking spray.
4. Return the Air Fryer Baskets to the Air Fryer.
5. Choose the Air Fryer mode for Zone 1 with 390 degrees F temperature and 17 minutes cooking time.
6. Select the "MATCH COOK" option to copy the settings for Zone 2.
7. Initiate cooking by pressing the START/PAUSE BUTTON.
8. Meanwhile, boil peas in hot water for 5 minutes until soft.
9. Then drain the peas and transfer them to the blender.
10. Add capers, lemon juice, and crème fraiche to the blender.
11. Blend until it makes a smooth mixture.
12. Spread the peas crème mixture on top of 2 lower halves of the bread roll, and place the fish fillets on it.
13. Place the remaining bread slices on top.
14. Serve fresh

Serving Suggestion: Serve with sautéed or fresh greens with melted butter.

Variation Tip: Coat the fish with crushed cornflakes for extra crispiness.

Nutritional Information Per Serving:
Calories 348 | Fat 30g |Sodium 660mg | Carbs 5g | Fiber 0g | Sugar 0g | Protein 14g

Fried Lobster Tails

Prep Time: 10 minutes.
Cook Time: 18 minutes.
Serves: 4

Ingredients:

- 4 (4 oz) lobster tails
- 8 tablespoons butter, melted
- 2 teaspoons lemon zest
- 2 garlic cloves, grated
- Salt and black pepper ground to taste
- 2 teaspoons fresh parsley, chopped
- 4 wedges lemon

Preparation:

1. Spread the lobster tails into Butterfly, slit the top to expose the lobster meat while keeping the tail intact.
2. Place two lobster tails in each of the Air Fryer baskets with their lobster meat facing up.
3. Mix melted butter with lemon zest and garlic in a bowl.
4. Brush the butter mixture on top of the lobster tails.
5. And drizzle salt and black pepper on top.
6. Return the Air Fryer Baskets to the Air Fryer.
7. Choose the Air Fryer mode for Zone 1 with 390 degrees F temperature and 18 minutes cooking time.
8. Select the "MATCH COOK" option to copy the settings for Zone 2.
9. Initiate cooking by pressing the START/PAUSE BUTTON.
10. Garnish with parsley and lemon wedges.
11. Serve warm

Serving Suggestion: Serve on a bed of lettuce leaves.

Variation Tip: Drizzle crushed cornflakes on top to have extra crispiness.

Nutritional Information Per Serving:

Calories 257 | Fat 10.4g |Sodium 431mg | Carbs 20g | Fiber 0g | Sugar 1.6g | Protein 21g

Buttered Mahi Mahi

Prep Time: 15 minutes.
Cook Time: 22 minutes.
Serves: 4

Ingredients:

- 4 (6 oz) mahi-mahi fillets
- Salt and black pepper ground to taste
- Cooking spray
- ⅔ cup butter

Preparation:

1. Preheat your Air Fryer Machine to 350 F.
2. Rub the Mahi-mahi fillets with salt and black pepper.
3. Place two mahi-mahi fillets in each of the Air Fryer's Basket.
4. Return the Air Fryer Baskets to the Air Fryer.
5. Choose the Air Fryer mode for Zone 1 with 390 degrees F temperature and 17 minutes cooking time.
6. Select the "MATCH COOK" option to copy the settings for Zone 2.
7. Initiate cooking by pressing the START/PAUSE BUTTON.
8. Add butter to a saucepan and cook for 5 minutes until slightly brown.
9. Remove the butter from the heat.
10. Drizzle butter over the fish and serve warm.

Serving Suggestion: Serve with pasta or fried rice.

Variation Tip: Drizzle parmesan cheese on top.

Nutritional Information Per Serving:
Calories 399 | Fat 16g |Sodium 537mg | Carbs 28g | Fiber 3g | Sugar 10g | Protein 35g

Salmon with Fennel Salad

Prep Time: 10 minutes.
Cook Time: 17 minutes.
Serves: 4

Ingredients:

- 2 teaspoons fresh parsley, chopped
- 1 teaspoon fresh thyme, chopped
- 1 teaspoon salt
- 4 (6-oz) skinless center-cut salmon fillets
- 2 tablespoons olive oil
- 4 cups fennel, sliced
- 2/3 cup Greek yogurt
- 1 garlic clove, grated
- 2 tablespoons orange juice
- 1 teaspoon lemon juice
- 2 tablespoons fresh dill, chopped

Preparation:

1. At 200 F, preheat your Air Fryer.
2. Mix ½ teaspoon salt, thyme, and parsley in a small bowl.
3. Brush the salmon with oil first, then rub liberally rub the herb mixture.
4. Place 2 salmon fillets in each of the Air fryer baskets.
5. Return the Air Fryer Baskets to the Air Fryer.
6. Choose the Air Fryer mode for Zone 1 with 390 degrees F temperature and 17 minutes cooking time.
7. Select the "MATCH COOK" option to copy the settings for Zone 2.
8. Initiate cooking by pressing the START/PAUSE BUTTON.
9. Meanwhile, mix fennel with garlic, yogurt, lemon juice, orange juice, remaining salt, and dill in a mixing bowl.
10. Serve the Air Fried Salmon fillets with fennel salad.
11. Enjoy.

Serving Suggestion: Serve with melted butter on top.

Variation Tip: Rub the salmon with lemon juice before cooking.

Nutritional Information Per Serving:

Calories 305 | Fat 15g |Sodium 482mg | Carbs 17g | Fiber 3g | Sugar 2g | Protein 35g

Savory Salmon Fillets

Prep Time: 10 minutes.
Cook Time: 17 minutes.
Serves: 4

Ingredients:

- 4 (6-oz) salmon fillets
- Salt, to taste
- Black pepper, to taste
- 4 teaspoons olive oil
- 4 tablespoons wholegrain mustard
- 2 tablespoons packed brown sugar
- 2 garlic cloves, minced
- 1 teaspoon thyme leaves

Preparation:

1. Rub the salmon with salt and black pepper first.
2. Whisk oil with sugar, thyme, garlic, and mustard in a small bowl.
3. Place two salmon fillets in each of the Air Fryer baskets and brush the thyme mixture on top of each fillet.
4. Return the Air Fryer Baskets to the Air Fryer.
5. Choose the Air Fryer mode for Zone 1 with 390 degrees F temperature and 17 minutes cooking time.
6. Select the "MATCH COOK" option to copy the settings for Zone 2.
7. Initiate cooking by pressing the START/PAUSE BUTTON.
8. Serve warm and fresh

Serving Suggestion: Serve with parsley and melted butter on top.

Variation Tip: Rub the fish fillets with lemon juice before cooking.

Nutritional Information Per Serving:
Calories 336 | Fat 6g |Sodium 181mg | Carbs 1.3g | Fiber 0.2g | Sugar 0.4g | Protein 69.2g

Crusted Cod

Prep Time: 15 minutes.
Cook Time: 13 minutes.
Serves: 4

Ingredients:

- 2 lbs cod fillets
- Salt, to taste
- Freshly black pepper, to taste
- ½ cup all-purpose flour
- 1 large egg, beaten
- 2 cups panko bread crumbs
- 1 teaspoon Old Bay seasoning
- Lemon wedges, for serving
- Tartar sauce, for serving

Preparation:

1. Rub the fish with salt and black pepper.
2. Add flour in one shallow bowl, beat eggs in another bowl, and mix panko with Old Bay in a shallow bowl.
3. First coat the fish with flour, then dip it in the eggs and finally coat it with the panko mixture.
4. Place half of the seasoned codfish in each Air Fryer basket.
5. Return the Air Fryer Baskets to the Air Fryer.
6. Choose the Air Fryer mode for Zone 1 with 390 degrees F temperature and 13 minutes cooking time.
7. Select the "MATCH COOK" option to copy the settings for Zone 2.
8. Initiate cooking by pressing the START/PAUSE BUTTON.
9. Flip the fish once cooked halfway, then resume cooking.
10. Serve warm and fresh with tartar sauce and lemon wedges.

Serving Suggestion: Enjoy with creamy coleslaw on the side.

Variation Tip: Use crushed cornflakes for extra crispiness.

Nutritional Information Per Serving:
Calories 155 | Fat 4.2g |Sodium 963mg | Carbs 21.5g | Fiber 0.8g | Sugar 5.7g | Protein 8.1g

Glazed Scallops

Prep Time: 15 minutes.
Cook Time: 13 minutes.
Serves: 6

Ingredients:

- 12 scallops
- 3 tablespoons olive oil
- Black pepper and salt to taste

Preparation:

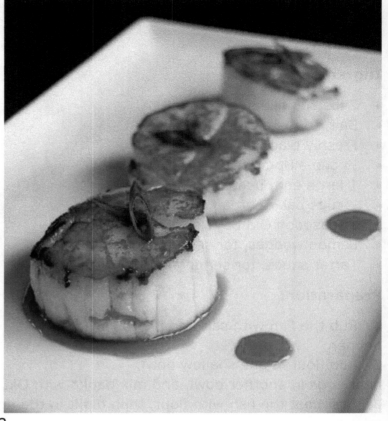

1. Rub the scallops with olive oil, black pepper, and salt.
2. Divide the scallops in the two Air fryer baskets.
3. Return the Air Fryer Baskets to the Air Fryer.
4. Choose the Air Fryer mode for Zone 1 with 390 degrees F temperature and 13 minutes cooking time.
5. Select the "MATCH COOK" option to copy the settings for Zone 2.
6. Initiate cooking by pressing the START/PAUSE BUTTON.
7. Flip the scallops once cooked halfway through, and resume cooking.
8. Serve warm

Serving Suggestion: Serve with melted butter on top.

Variation Tip: Drizzle breadcrumbs on top before Air Frying.

Nutritional Information Per Serving:
Calories 308 | Fat 24g |Sodium 715mg | Carbs 0.8g | Fiber 0.1g | Sugar 0.1g | Protein 21.9g

Crusted Tilapia

Prep Time: 20 minutes.
Cook Time: 17 minutes.
Serves: 4

Ingredients:

- 3/4 cup breadcrumbs
- 1 packet dry ranch-style dressing
- 2 1/2 tablespoons vegetable oil
- 2 eggs beaten
- 4 tilapia fillets
- Herbs and chilies to garnish

Preparation:

1. Thoroughly mix ranch dressing with panko in a bowl.
2. Whisk eggs in a shallow bowl.
3. Dip each fish fillet in the egg, then coat evenly with the panko mixture.
4. Set two coated fillets in each of the Air Fryer baskets.
5. Return the Air Fryer Baskets to the Air Fryer.
6. Choose the Air Fryer mode for Zone 1 with 390 degrees F temperature and 17 minutes cooking time.
7. Select the "MATCH COOK" option to copy the settings for Zone 2.
8. Initiate cooking by pressing the START/PAUSE BUTTON.
9. Serve warm with herbs and chilies

Serving Suggestion: Serve with sautéed asparagus on the side.

Variation Tip: Coat the fish with crushed cornflakes for extra crispiness.

Nutritional Information Per Serving:
Calories 196 | Fat 7.1g |Sodium 492mg | Carbs 21.6g | Fiber 2.9g | Sugar 0.8g | Protein 13.4g

Crispy Catfish

Prep Time: 15 minutes.
Cook Time: 17 minutes.
Serves: 4

Ingredients:

- 4 catfish fillets
- 1/4 cup Louisiana Fish fry
- 1 tablespoon olive oil
- 1 tablespoon parsley, chopped
- 1 lemon, sliced
- Fresh herbs, to garnish

Preparation:

1. Mix fish fry with olive oil, and parsley then liberally rub over the catfish.
2. Place two fillets in each of the Air fryer baskets.
3. Return the Air Fryer Baskets to the Air Fryer.
4. Choose the Air Fryer mode for Zone 1 with 390 degrees F temperature and 17 minutes cooking time.
5. Select the "MATCH COOK" option to copy the settings for Zone 2.
6. Initiate cooking by pressing the START/PAUSE BUTTON.
7. Garnish with lemon slices and herbs.
8. Serve warm

Serving Suggestion: Serve with creamy dip and crispy fries.

Variation Tip: Use crushed cornflakes for breading to have extra crispiness.

Nutritional Information Per Serving:

Calories 275 | Fat 1.4g |Sodium 582mg | Carbs 31.5g | Fiber 1.1g | Sugar 0.1g | Protein 29.8g

Salmon Nuggets

Prep Time: 15 minutes.
Cook Time: 15 minutes.
Serves: 4

Ingredients:

- ⅓ cup maple syrup
- ¼ teaspoon dried chipotle pepper
- 1 pinch sea salt
- 1 ½ cups croutons
- 1 large egg
- 1 (1 pound) skinless salmon fillet, cut into 1 1/2-inch chunk
- cooking spray

Preparation:

1. Mix chipotle powder, maple syrup, and salt in a saucepan and cook on a simmer for 5 minutes.
2. Crush the croutons in a food processor and transfer to a bowl.
3. Beat egg in another shallow bowl.
4. Season the salmon chunks with sea salt.
5. Dip the salmon in the egg, then coat with breadcrumbs.
6. Divide the coated salmon chunks in the two Air fryer baskets.
7. Return the Air Fryer Baskets to the Air Fryer.
8. Select the Air Fryer mode for Zone 1 with 390 degrees F temperature and 10 minutes cooking time.
9. Press the "MATCH COOK" button to copy the settings for Zone 2.
10. Initiate cooking by pressing the START/PAUSE BUTTON.
11. Flip the chunks once cooked halfway through, then resume cooking.
12. Pour the maple syrup on top and serve warm.

Serving Suggestion: Serve with creamy dip and crispy fries.

Variation Tip: Use crushed cornflakes for breading to have extra crispiness.

Nutritional Information Per Serving:

Calories 275 | Fat 1.4g |Sodium 582mg | Carbs 31.5g | Fiber 1.1g | Sugar 0.1g | Protein 29.8g

Breaded Scallops

Prep Time: 15 minutes.
Cook Time: 12 minutes.
Serves: 4

Ingredients:

- ½ cup crushed buttery crackers
- ½ teaspoon garlic powder
- ½ teaspoon seafood seasoning
- 2 tablespoons butter, melted
- 1-pound sea scallops patted dry
- cooking spray

Preparation:

1. Mix cracker crumbs, garlic powder, and seafood seasoning in a shallow bowl. Spread melted butter in another shallow bowl.
2. Dip each scallop in the melted butter and then roll in the breading to coat well.
3. Grease each Air fryer basket with cooking spray and place half of the scallops in each.
4. Return the Air Fryer Baskets to the Air Fryer.
5. Select the Air Fryer mode for Zone 1 with 390 degrees F temperature and 12 minutes cooking time.
6. Press the "MATCH COOK" button to copy the settings for Zone 2.
7. Initiate cooking by pressing the START/PAUSE BUTTON.
8. Flip the scallops with a spatula after 4 minutes and resume cooking.
9. Serve warm.

Serving Suggestion: Serve with creamy dip and crispy fries.

Variation Tip: Use crushed cornflakes for breading to have extra crispiness.

Nutritional Information Per Serving:

Calories 275 | Fat 1.4g |Sodium 582mg | Carbs 31.5g | Fiber 1.1g | Sugar 0.1g | Protein 29.8g

Poultry Mains Recipes

Crumbed Chicken Katsu

Prep Time: 15 minutes.
Cook Time: 26 minutes.
Serves: 4

Ingredients:
- 1 lb boneless chicken breast, cut in half
- 2 large eggs, beaten
- 1 ½ cups panko bread crumbs
- Salt and black pepper ground to taste
- Cooking spray

Sauce:
- 1 tablespoon sugar
- 2 tablespoons soy sauce
- 1 tablespoon sherry
- ½ cup ketchup

- 2 teaspoons Worcestershire sauce
- 1 teaspoon garlic, minced

Preparation:
1. Mix soy sauce, ketchup, sherry, sugar, garlic, and Worcestershire sauce in a mixing bowl.
2. Keep this katsu aside for a while.
3. Rub the chicken pieces with salt and black pepper.
4. Whisk eggs in a shallow dish and spread breadcrumbs in another tray.
5. Dip the chicken in the egg mixture and coat them with breadcrumbs.
6. Place the coated chicken in the two Air Fryer Baskets and spray them with cooking spray.
7. Return the Air Fryer Baskets to the Air Fryer.
8. Choose the Air Fryer mode for Zone 1 with 390 degrees F temperature and 26 minutes cooking time.
9. Select the "MATCH COOK" option to copy the settings for Zone 2.
10. Initiate cooking by pressing the START/PAUSE BUTTON.
11. Flip the chicken once cooked halfway through, then resume cooking.
12. Serve warm with the sauce

Serving Suggestion: Serve with fried rice and green beans salad.
Variation Tip: Coat the chicken with crushed cornflakes for extra crispiness.
Nutritional Information Per Serving:
Calories 220 | Fat 1.7g | Sodium 178mg | Carbs 1.7g | Fiber 0.2g | Sugar 0.2g | Protein 32.9g

Bacon-Wrapped Chicken

Prep Time: 10 minutes.
Cook Time: 28 minutes.
Serves: 2

Ingredients:

- Butter:
- ½ stick butter softened
- ½ garlic clove, minced
- ¼ teaspoons dried thyme
- ¼ teaspoons dried basil
- ⅛ teaspoons coarse salt
- 1 pinch black pepper, ground
- ⅓ lb thick-cut bacon
- 1 ½ lbs boneless skinless
chicken thighs
- 2 teaspoons garlic, minced

Preparation:

1. Mix garlic softened butter with thyme, salt, basil, and black pepper in a bowl.
2. Add butter mixture on a piece of wax paper and roll it up tightly to make a butter log.
3. Place the log in the refrigerator for 2 hours.
4. Spray one bacon strip on a piece of wax paper.
5. Place each chicken thigh on top of one bacon strip and rub it with garlic.
6. Make a slit in the chicken thigh and add a teaspoon of butter to the chicken.
7. Wrap the bacon around the chicken thigh.
8. Repeat those same steps with all the chicken thighs.
9. Place the bacon-wrapped chicken thighs in the two Air Fryer Baskets.
10. Return the Air Fryer Baskets to the Air Fryer.
11. Choose the Air Fryer mode for Zone 1 with 390 degrees F temperature and 28 minutes cooking time.
12. Select the "MATCH COOK" option to copy the settings for Zone 2.
13. Initiate cooking by pressing the START/PAUSE BUTTON.
14. Flip the chicken once cooked halfway through, and resume cooking.
15. Serve warm

Serving Suggestion: Serve with tomato ketchup or chili sauce.

Variation Tip: Drizzle mixed dried herbs on top before cooking.

Nutritional Information Per Serving:
Calories 380 | Fat 29g | Sodium 821mg | Carbs 34.6g | Fiber 0g | Sugar 0g | Protein 30g

Bang-Bang Chicken

Prep Time: 15 minutes.
Cook Time: 20 minutes.
Serves: 2

Ingredients:

- 1 cup mayonnaise
- ½ cup sweet chili sauce
- 2 tablespoons Sriracha sauce
- ⅓ cup flour
- 1 lb boneless chicken breast, diced
- 1 ½ cups panko bread crumbs
- 2 green onions, chopped

Preparation:

1. Mix mayonnaise with Sriracha and sweet chili sauce in a large bowl.
2. Keep 3/4 cup of the mixture aside.
3. Add flour, chicken, breadcrumbs, and remaining mayo mixture to a resealable plastic bag.
4. Zip the bag and shake well to coat.
5. Divide the chicken in the two Air fryer baskets in a single layer.
6. Return the Air Fryer Baskets to the Air Fryer.
7. Choose the Air Fryer mode for Zone 1 with 390 degrees F temperature and 20 minutes cooking time.
8. Select the "MATCH COOK" option to copy the settings for Zone 2.
9. Initiate cooking by pressing the START/PAUSE BUTTON.
10. Flip the chicken once cooked halfway through.
11. Top the chicken with reserved mayo sauce.
12. Garnish with green onions and serve warm

Serving Suggestion: Serve with tomato ketchup or chili sauce.

Variation Tip: Use crushed cornflakes for breading to have extra crispiness.

Nutritional Information Per Serving:

Calories 374 | Fat 13g |Sodium 552mg | Carbs 25g | Fiber 1.2g | Sugar 1.2g | Protein 37.7g

General Tso's Chicken

Prep Time: 20 minutes.
Cook Time: 22 minutes.
Serves: 4

Ingredients:

- 1 egg, large
- 1/3 cup 2 teaspoons cornstarch,
- 1/4 teaspoons salt
- 1/4 teaspoons ground white pepper
- 7 tablespoons chicken broth
- 2 tablespoons soy sauce
- 2 tablespoons ketchup
- 2 teaspoons sugar
- 2 teaspoons unseasoned rice vinegar
- 1 1/2 tablespoons canola oil
- 4 chilies de árbol, chopped and seeds discarded
- 1 tablespoon chopped fresh ginger
- 1 tablespoon garlic, chopped
- 2 tablespoons green onion, sliced
- 1 teaspoon toasted sesame oil
- 1 lb boneless chicken thighs, cut into 1 ¼ -inch chunks
- 1/2 teaspoons toasted sesame seeds

Preparation:

1. Add egg to a large bowl and beat it with a fork.
2. Add chicken to the egg and coat it well.
3. Whisk 1/3 cup cornstarch with black pepper and salt in a small bowl.
4. Add chicken to the cornstarch mixture and mix well to coat.
5. Divide the chicken in the two air fryer baskets and spray them cooking oi.
6. Return the Air Fryer Baskets to the Air Fryer.
7. Choose the Air Fryer mode for Zone 1 with 390 degrees F temperature and 20 minutes cooking time.
8. Select the "MATCH COOK" option to copy the settings for Zone 2.
9. Initiate cooking by pressing the START/PAUSE BUTTON.
10. Once done, remove the air fried chicken from the Air fryer.

11. Whisk 2 teaspoons cornstarch with soy sauce, broth, sugar, ketchup, and rice vinegar in a small bowl.
12. Add chilies and canola oil to a skillet and sauté for 1 minute.
13. Add garlic and ginger, then sauté for 30 seconds.
14. Stir in cornstarch sauce and cook until it bubbles and thickens.
15. Toss in cooked chicken and garnish with sesame oil, sesame seeds, and green onion.
16. Enjoy.

Serving Suggestion: Serve with boiled white rice or chow Mein.

Variation Tip: You can use honey instead of sugar to sweeten the sauce.

Nutritional Information Per Serving:
Calories 351 | Fat 16g |Sodium 777mg | Carbs 26g | Fiber 4g | Sugar 5g | Protein 28g

Chicken Drumettes

Prep Time: 15 minutes.
Cook Time: 52 minutes.
Serves: 5

Ingredients:

- 10 large chicken drumettes
- Cooking spray
- ¼ cup of rice vinegar
- 3 tablespoons honey
- 2 tablespoons unsalted chicken stock
- 1 tablespoon soy sauce
- 1 tablespoon toasted sesame oil
- 3/8 teaspoons crushed red pepper
- 1 garlic clove, chopped
- 2 tablespoons chopped unsalted roasted peanuts
- 1 tablespoon chopped fresh chives

Preparation:

1. Spread the chicken in the two Air Fryer Baskets in an even layer and spray cooking spray on top.
2. Return the Air Fryer Baskets to the Air Fryer.
3. Choose the Air Fryer mode for Zone 1 with 390 degrees F temperature and 47 minutes cooking time.
4. Select the "MATCH COOK" option to copy the settings for Zone 2.
5. Initiate cooking by pressing the START/PAUSE BUTTON.
6. Flip the chicken drumettes once cooked halfway through, then resume cooking.
7. During this time, mix soy sauce, honey, stock, vinegar, garlic, and crushed red pepper in a suitable saucepan and place it over medium-high heat to cook on a simmer.
8. Cook this sauce for 6 minutes with occasional stirring, then pour it into a medium-sized bowl.
9. Add Air fried drumettes and toss well to coat with the honey sauce.
10. Garnish with chives and peanuts.
11. Serve warm and fresh

Serving Suggestion: Serve with tomato ketchup or chili sauce.

Variation Tip: Rub the chicken with lemon juice before seasoning.

Nutritional Information Per Serving:

Calories 268 | Fat 10.4g |Sodium 411mg | Carbs 0.4g | Fiber 0.1g | Sugar 0.1g | Protein 40.6g

Crusted Chicken Breast

Prep Time: 15 minutes.
Cook Time: 28 minutes.
Serves: 4

Ingredients:

- 2 large eggs, beaten
- 1/2 cup all-purpose flour
- 1 1/4 cup panko bread crumbs
- 2/3 cup Parmesan, grated
- 4 teaspoons lemon zest
- 2 teaspoons dried oregano
- Salt, to taste
- 1 teaspoon cayenne pepper
- Freshly black pepper, to taste
- 4 boneless skinless chicken breasts

Preparation:

1. Beat eggs in one shallow bowl and spread flour in another shallow bowl.
2. Mix panko with oregano, lemon zest, Parmesan, cayenne, oregano, salt, and black pepper in another shallow bowl.
3. First, coat the chicken with flour first, then dip it in the eggs and coat them with panko mixture.
4. Arrange the prepared chicken in the two Air Fryer Baskets.
5. Return the Air Fryer Baskets to the Air Fryer.
6. Choose the Air Fryer mode for Zone 1 with 390 degrees F temperature and 28 minutes cooking time.
7. Select the "MATCH COOK" option to copy the settings for Zone 2.
8. Initiate cooking by pressing the START/PAUSE BUTTON.
9. Flip the half-cooked chicken and continue cooking for 5 minutes until golden.
10. Serve warm

Serving Suggestion: Serve with fresh-cut tomatoes and sautéed greens.

Variation Tip: Rub the chicken with lemon juice before seasoning.

Nutritional Information Per Serving:

Calories 220 | Fat 13g |Sodium 542mg | Carbs 0.9g | Fiber 0.3g | Sugar 0.2g | Protein 25.6g

Pickled Chicken Fillets

Prep Time: 15 minutes.
Cook Time: 28 minutes.
Serves: 4

Ingredients:

- 2 boneless chicken breasts
- 1/2 cup dill pickle juice
- 2 eggs
- 1/2 cup milk
- 1 cup flour, all-purpose
- 2 tablespoons powdered sugar
- 2 tablespoons potato starch
- 1 teaspoon paprika
- 1 teaspoon of sea salt
- 1/2 teaspoons black pepper
- 1/2 teaspoons garlic powder
- 1/4 teaspoons ground celery seed ground
- 1 tablespoon olive oil
- Cooking spray
- 4 hamburger buns, toasted
- 8 dill pickle chips

Preparation:

1. Set the chicken in a suitable Ziplock bag and pound it into ½ thickness with a mallet.
2. Slice the chicken into 2 halves.
3. Add pickle juice and seal the bag.
4. Refrigerate for 30 minutes approximately for marination. Whisk both eggs with milk in a shallow bowl.
5. Thoroughly mix flour with spices and flour in a separate bowl.
6. Dip each chicken slice in egg, then in the flour mixture.
7. Shake off the excess and set the chicken pieces in the Air Fryer basket.
8. Spray the pieces with cooking oil.
9. Place the chicken pieces in the two air fryer baskets in a single layer and spray the cooking oil.
10. Return the Air Fryer Baskets to the Air Fryer.
11. Choose the Air Fryer mode for Zone 1 with 390 degrees F temperature and 28 minutes cooking time.
12. Select the "MATCH COOK" option to copy the settings for Zone 2.
13. Initiate cooking by pressing the START/PAUSE BUTTON.
14. Flip the chicken pieces once cooked halfway through, and resume cooking.
15. Enjoy with pickle chips and a dollop of mayonnaise.

Serving Suggestion: Serve with warm corn tortilla and Greek salad.

Variation Tip: You can use the almond flour breading for low-carb serving.

Nutritional Information Per Serving:
Calories 353 | Fat 5g |Sodium 818mg | Carbs 53.2g | Fiber 4.4g | Sugar 8g | Protein 17.3g

Chicken Potatoes

Prep Time: 10 minutes.
Cook Time: 22 minutes.
Serves: 4

Ingredients:

- 15 ounces canned potatoes drained
- 1 teaspoon olive oil
- 1 teaspoon Lawry's seasoned salt
- 1/8 teaspoons black pepper optional
- 8 ounces boneless chicken breast cubed
- 1/4 teaspoons paprika
- 3/8 cup cheddar, shredded
- 4 bacon slices, cooked, cut into strips

Preparation:

1. Dice the chicken into small pieces and toss them with olive oil and spices.
2. Drain and dice the potato pieces into smaller cubes.
3. Add potato to the chicken and mix well to coat.
4. Spread the mixture in the two Air fryer baskets in a single layer.
5. Return the Air Fryer Baskets to the Air Fryer.
6. Choose the Air Fryer mode for Zone 1 with 390 degrees F temperature and 22 minutes cooking time.
7. Select the "MATCH COOK" option to copy the settings for Zone 2.
8. Initiate cooking by pressing the START/PAUSE BUTTON.
9. Top the chicken and potatoes with cheese and bacon.
10. Return the Air Fryer Baskets to the Air Fryer.
11. Select the Air Broil mode for Zone 1 with 300 degrees F temperature and 5 minutes cooking time.
12. Initiate cooking by pressing the START/PAUSE BUTTON.
13. Repeat the same step for ZONE 2 to broil the potatoes and chicken in the 2nd basket.
14. Enjoy with dried herbs on top.

Serving Suggestion: Serve with boiled white rice.

Variation Tip: Add sweet potatoes and green beans instead of potatoes.

Nutritional Information Per Serving:

Calories 346 | Fat 16.1g |Sodium 882mg | Carbs 1.3g | Fiber 0.5g | Sugar 0.5g | Protein 48.2g

Air Fried Turkey Breast

Prep Time: 10 minutes.
Cook Time: 46 minutes.
Serves: 4

Ingredients:

- 2 lbs. turkey breast, on the bone with skin
- ½ tablespoons olive oil
- 1 teaspoon salt
- 1/4 tablespoons dry poultry seasoning

Preparation:

1. Rub turkey breast with ½ tablespoons oil.
2. Season both its sides with turkey seasoning and salt, then rub in the brush half tablespoons of oil over the skin of the turkey.
3. Divide the turkey in half and place each half in each of the Air fryer baskets.
4. Return the Air Fryer Baskets to the Air Fryer.
5. Choose the Air Fryer mode for Zone 1 with 390 degrees F temperature and 46 minutes cooking time.
6. Select the "MATCH COOK" option to copy the settings for Zone 2.
7. Initiate cooking by pressing the START/PAUSE BUTTON.
8. Flip the turkey once cooked halfway through, and resume cooking.
9. Slice and serve warm.

Serving Suggestion: Serve with warm corn tortilla and Greek salad.

Variation Tip: Coat and dust the turkey breast with flour after seasoning.

Nutritional Information Per Serving:
Calories 502 | Fat 25g |Sodium 230mg | Carbs 1.5g | Fiber 0.2g | Sugar 0.4g | Protein 64.1g

Chili Chicken Wings

Prep Time: 20 minutes.
Cook Time: 43 minutes.
Serves: 4

Ingredients:

* 8 chicken wings drumettes
* cooking spray
* 1/8 cup low-fat buttermilk
* 1/4 cup almond flour
* McCormick Chicken Seasoning
to taste

Thai Chili Marinade

* 1 1/2 tablespoons low-sodium
soy sauce
* ½ teaspoon ginger, minced
* 1 1/2 garlic cloves
* 1 green onion
* ½ teaspoon of rice wine vinegar
* ½ tablespoons Sriracha sauce
* ½ tablespoons sesame oil

Preparation:

1. Put all the ingredients for the marinade in the blender and blend them for 1 minute.
2. Keep this marinade aside. Pat dry the washed chicken and place it in the Ziploc bag.
3. Add buttermilk, chicken seasoning, and zip the bag.
4. Shake the bag well, then refrigerator for 30 minutes for marination.
5. Remove the chicken drumettes from the marinade, then dredge them through dry flour.
6. Spread the drumettes in the two air fryer baskets and spray them with cooking oil.
7. Return the Air Fryer Baskets to the Air Fryer.
8. Choose the Air Fryer mode for Zone 1 with 390 degrees F temperature and 43 minutes cooking time.
9. Select the "MATCH COOK" option to copy the settings for Zone 2.
10. Initiate cooking by pressing the START/PAUSE BUTTON.
11. Toss the drumettes once cooked halfway through.

12.Now brush the chicken pieces with Thai chili sauce and then resume cooking
13.Serve warm

Serving Suggestion: Serve with warm corn tortilla and ketchup.

Variation Tip: Rub the wings with lemon or orange juice before cooking.

Nutritional Information Per Serving:
Calories 223 | Fat 11.7g |Sodium 721mg | Carbs 13.6g | Fiber 0.7g | Sugar 8g | Protein 15.7g

Brazilian Chicken Drumsticks

Prep Time: 15 minutes.
Cook Time: 47 minutes.
Serves: 6

Ingredients:

- 2 teaspoons cumin seeds
- 2 teaspoons dried parsley
- 2 teaspoons turmeric powder
- 2 teaspoons dried oregano leaves
- 2 teaspoons salt
- 1 teaspoon coriander seeds
- 1 teaspoon black peppercorns
- 1 teaspoon cayenne pepper
- 1/2 cup lime juice
- 4 tablespoons vegetable oil
- 3 lbs chicken drumsticks

Preparation:

1. Grind cumin, parsley, salt, coriander seeds, cayenne pepper, peppercorns, oregano, and turmeric in a food processor.
2. Add this mixture to lemon juice and oil in a bowl and mix well.
3. Rub the spice paste over the chicken drumsticks and let them marinate for 30 minutes.
4. Divide the chicken drumsticks in both the Air Fryer Baskets.
5. Return the Air Fryer Baskets to the Air Fryer.
6. Choose the Air Fryer mode for Zone 1 with 390 degrees F temperature and 47 minutes cooking time.
7. Select the "MATCH COOK" option to copy the settings for Zone 2.
8. Initiate cooking by pressing the START/PAUSE BUTTON.
9. Flip the drumsticks when cooked halfway through, then resume cooking.
10. Serve warm.

Serving Suggestion: Serve with tomato ketchup or chili sauce.

Variation Tip: Use buttermilk to soak the drumsticks before seasoning.

Nutritional Information Per Serving:
Calories 456 | Fat 16.4g |Sodium 1321mg | Carbs 19.2g | Fiber 2.2g | Sugar 4.2g | Protein 55.2g

Balsamic Duck Breast

Prep Time: 15 minutes.
Cook Time: 20 minutes.
Serves: 2

Ingredients:

- 2 Duck Breasts
- 1 teaspoon parsley
- Salt and black pepper, to taste

Marinade:

- 1 tablespoon olive oil
- ½ teaspoon French mustard
- 1 teaspoon dried garlic
- 2 teaspoons honey
- ½ teaspoon Balsamic vinegar

Preparation:

1. Mix olive oil, mustard, garlic, honey, and balsamic vinegar in a bowl.
2. Add duck breasts to the marinade and rub well.
3. Place one duck breast in each air fryer basket.
4. Return the Air Fryer Baskets to the Air Fryer.
5. Choose the Air Fryer mode for Zone 1 with 360 degrees F temperature and 20 minutes cooking time.
6. Select the "MATCH COOK" option to copy the settings for Zone 2.
7. Initiate cooking by pressing the START/PAUSE BUTTON.
8. Flip the duck breasts once cooked halfway through, then resume cooking.
9. Serve warm.

Serving Suggestion: Serve with white rice and avocado salad

Variation Tip: Rub the duck breast with garlic cloves before seasoning.

Nutritional Information Per Serving:

Calories 546 | Fat 33.1g |Sodium 1201mg | Carbs 30g | Fiber 2.4g | Sugar 9.7g | Protein 32g

Cheddar- Stuffed Chicken

Prep Time: 10 minutes.
Cook Time: 20 minutes.
Serves: 4

Ingredients:

- 3 bacon strips, cooked and crumbled
- 2 ounces Cheddar cheese, cubed
- ¼ cup barbeque sauce
- 2 (4 ounces) boneless chicken breasts
- Salt and black pepper to taste

Preparation:

1. Make a 1-inch deep pouch in each chicken breast.
2. Mix cheddar cubes with half of the BBQ sauce, salt, black pepper, and bacon.
3. Divide this filling in the chicken breasts and secure the edges with a toothpick.
4. Brush the remaining BBQ sauce over the chicken breasts.
5. Place the chicken in Air fryer basket 1 and spray them with cooking oil.
6. Return the Air Fryer Basket to the Air Fryer.
7. Choose the Air Fryer mode for Zone 1 with 360 degrees F temperature and 20 minutes cooking time.
8. Initiate cooking by pressing the START/PAUSE BUTTON.
9. Serve warm.

Serving Suggestion: Serve with tomato salsa on top.

Variation Tip: Use poultry seasoning for breading.

Nutritional Information Per Serving:

Calories 379 | Fat 19g |Sodium 184mg | Carbs 12.3g | Fiber 0.6g | Sugar 2g | Protein 37.7g

Veggie Stuffed Chicken Breasts

Prep Time: 15 minutes.
Cook Time: 10 minutes.
Serves: 2

Ingredients:

- 4 teaspoons chili powder
- 4 teaspoons ground cumin
- 1 skinless, boneless chicken breast
- 2 teaspoons chipotle flakes
- 2 teaspoons Mexican oregano
- Salt and black pepper, to taste
- ½ red bell pepper, julienned
- ½ onion, julienned
- 1 fresh jalapeno pepper, julienned
- 2 teaspoons corn oil
- ½ lime, juiced

Preparation:

1. Slice the chicken breast in half horizontally.
2. Pound each chicken breast with a mallet into ¼ inch thickness.
3. Rub the pounded chicken breast with black pepper, salt, oregano, chipotle flakes, cumin, and chili powder.
4. Add ½ of bell pepper, jalapeno, and onion on top of each chicken breast piece.
5. Roll the chicken to wrap the filling inside and insert toothpicks to seal.
6. Place the rolls in Air fryer basket 1 and spray them with cooking oil.
7. Return the Air Fryer Basket to the Air Fryer.
8. Choose the Air Fryer mode for Zone 1 with 360 degrees F temperature and 10 minutes cooking time.
9. Initiate cooking by pressing the START/PAUSE BUTTON.
10. Serve warm.

Serving Suggestion: Serve with tomato ketchup or chili sauce.

Variation Tip: season the chicken rolls with seasoned parmesan before cooking.

Nutritional Information Per Serving:
Calories 351 | Fat 11g |Sodium 150mg | Carbs 3.3g | Fiber 0.2g | Sugar 1g | Protein 33.2g

Beef, Pork, and Lamb Recipes

Pork with Green Beans and Potatoes

Prep Time: 10 minutes.
Cook Time: 15 minutes.
Serves: 4

Ingredients:
- ¼ cup Dijon mustard
- 2 tablespoons brown sugar
- 1 teaspoon dried parsley flake
- ½ teaspoon dried thyme
- ¼ teaspoons salt
- ¼ teaspoons black pepper
- 1 ¼ lb pork tenderloin
- ¾ lb small potatoes halved
- 1 (12 oz) package green beans, trimmed
- 1 tablespoon olive oil
- Salt and black pepper ground to taste

Preparation:
1. Preheat your Air Fryer Machine to 400 F.
2. Add mustard, parsley, brown sugar, salt, black pepper, and thyme in a large bowl, then mix well.
3. Add tenderloin to the spice mixture and coat well.
4. Toss potatoes with olive oil, salt, black pepper, and green beans in another bowl.
5. Place the prepared tenderloin in Zone 1 Basket.
6. Return this Air Fryer Basket to the Air Fryer.
7. Choose the Air Fryer mode for Zone 1 with 390 degrees F temperature and 15 minutes cooking time.
8. Add potatoes and green beans to the second Basket
9. Choose the Air Fryer mode for Zone 2 with 350 degrees F temperature and 10 minutes cooking time.
10. Press the SMART FINISH button to sync the settings with Zone 2.
11. Initiate cooking by pressing the START/PAUSE BUTTON.
12. Serve the tenderloin with Air Fried potatoes

Serving Suggestion: Serve with sautéed leeks or cabbages.
Variation Tip: Rub the tenderloins with garlic cloves before seasoning.
Nutritional Information Per Serving:
Calories 400 | Fat 32g |Sodium 721mg | Carbs 2.6g | Fiber 0g | Sugar 0g | Protein 27.4g

Air Fryer Meatloaves

Prep Time: 10 minutes.
Cook Time: 22 minutes.
Serves: 4

Ingredients:

- ⅓ cup milk
- 2 tablespoons basil pesto
- 1 egg, beaten
- 1 garlic clove, minced
- ¼ teaspoons black pepper
- 1 lb ground beef
- ⅓ cup panko bread crumbs
- 8 pepperoni slices
- ½ cup marinara sauce, warmed
- 1 tablespoon fresh basil, chopped

Preparation:

1. Mix pesto, milk, egg, garlic, and black pepper in a medium-sized bowl.
2. Stir in ground beef and bread crumbs, then mix.
3. Make the 4 small-sized loaves with this mixture and top them with 2 pepperoni slices.
4. Press the slices into the meatloaves.
5. Place the meatloaves in the two Air Fryer Baskets.
6. Return the Air Fryer Baskets to the Air Fryer.
7. Choose the Air Fryer mode for Zone 1 with 390 degrees F temperature and 22 minutes cooking time.
8. Select the "MATCH COOK" option to copy the settings for Zone 2.
9. Initiate cooking by pressing the START/PAUSE BUTTON.
10. Top them with marinara sauce and basil to serve.
11. Serve warm.

Serving Suggestion: Serve with avocado dip.

Variation Tip: Add finely chopped carrots and zucchini to the meatloaf.

Nutritional Information Per Serving:

Calories 316 | Fat 12.2g |Sodium 587mg | Carbs 12.2g | Fiber 1g | Sugar 1.8g | Protein 25.8g

Pork Chops with Brussels Sprouts

Prep Time: 15 minutes.
Cook Time: 15 minutes.
Serves: 4

Ingredients:

- 4 bone-in center-cut pork chop
- Cooking spray
- Salt, to taste
- Black pepper, to taste
- 2 teaspoons olive oil
- 2 teaspoons pure maple syrup
- 2 teaspoons Dijon mustard
- 6 ounces Brussels sprouts, quartered

Preparation:

1. Rub pork chop with salt, ¼ teaspoons black pepper, and cooking spray.
2. Toss brussels sprouts with mustard, syrup, oil, ¼ teaspoons black pepper in a medium bowl.
3. Add pork chop to the Zone 1 basket of the Air fryer.
4. Return the Air Fryer Basket to the Air Fryer.
5. Choose the Air Fryer mode for Zone 1 with 400 degrees F temperature and 15 minutes cooking time.
6. Add the brussels sprouts to the Zone 2 basket and return it to the unit.
7. Choose the Air Fryer mode for Zone 2 with 350 degrees F temperature and 13 minutes cooking time.
8. Press the SMART FINISH button to sync the settings with Zone 2.
9. Initiate cooking by pressing the START/PAUSE BUTTON.
10. Serve warm and fresh

Serving Suggestion: Serve with Greek salad and crispy bread.

Variation Tip: Rub the pork chops with garlic cloves before seasoning.

Nutritional Information Per Serving:

Calories 336 | Fat 27.1g |Sodium 66mg | Carbs 1.1g | Fiber 0.4g | Sugar 0.2g | Protein 19.7g

Turkey and Beef Meatballs

Prep Time: 15 minutes.
Cook Time: 24 minutes.
Serves: 6

Ingredients:

- 1 medium shallot, minced
- 2 tablespoons olive oil
- 3 garlic cloves, minced
- 1/4 cup panko crumbs
- 2 tablespoons whole milk
- 2/3 lb lean ground beef
- 1/3 lb bulk turkey sausage
- 1 large egg, lightly beaten
- ¼ cup parsley, chopped
- 1 tablespoon fresh thyme, chopped
- 1 tablespoon fresh rosemary, chopped
- 1 tablespoon Dijon mustard
- ½ teaspoon salt

Preparation:

1. At 400 F, preheat your oven. Place a medium non-stick pan over medium-high heat.
2. Add oil and shallot, then sauté for 2 minutes.
3. Toss in the garlic and cook for 1 minute.
4. Remove this pan from the heat.
5. Whisk panko with milk in a large bowl and leave it for 5 minutes.
6. Add cooked shallot mixture and mix well.
7. Stir in egg, parsley, turkey sausage, beef, thyme, rosemary, salt, and mustard.
8. Mix well, then divide the mixture into 1 ½ inches balls.
9. Divide these balls into the two Air fryer baskets and spray them with cooking oil.
10. Return the Air Fryer Baskets to the Air Fryer.
11. Choose the Air Fryer mode for Zone 1 with 400 degrees F temperature and 21 minutes cooking time.
12. Select the "MATCH COOK" option to copy the settings for Zone 2.
13. Initiate cooking by pressing the START/PAUSE BUTTON.
14. Serve warm

Serving Suggestion: Serve with fresh vegetable salad and marinara sauce.

Variation Tip: Add freshly chopped parsley and coriander for change of taste.

Nutritional Information Per Serving:
Calories 551 | Fat 31g |Sodium 1329mg | Carbs 1.5g | Fiber 0.8g | Sugar 0.4g | Protein 64g

Pork Chops with Broccoli

Prep Time: 15 minutes.
Cook Time: 13 minutes.
Serves: 2

Ingredients:

- 2 (5 ounces) bone-in pork chops
- 2 tablespoons avocado oil
- 1/2 teaspoon paprika
- 1/2 teaspoon onion powder
- ½ teaspoon garlic powder
- 1 teaspoon salt
- 2 cups broccoli florets
- 2 garlic cloves, minced

Preparation:

1. Rub the pork chops with avocado oil, garlic, paprika, and spices.
2. Add pork chop to the Zone 1 basket of the Air fryer.
3. Return the Air Fryer Basket to the Air Fryer.
4. Choose the Air Fryer mode for Zone 1 with 400 degrees F temperature and 12 minutes cooking time.
5. Add the broccoli to the Zone 2 basket and return it to the unit.
6. Choose the Air Fryer mode for Zone 2 with 375 degrees F temperature and 13 minutes cooking time.
7. Press the SMART FINISH button to sync the settings with Zone 2.
8. Initiate cooking by pressing the START/PAUSE BUTTON.
9. Flip the pork once cooked halfway through.
10. Cut the hardened butter into the cubes and place them on top of the pork chops.
11. Serve warm with crispy broccoli florets

Serving Suggestion: Serve with warm corn tortilla and crouton salad.

Variation Tip: Rub the pork chops with garlic cloves before seasoning.

Nutritional Information Per Serving:

Calories 410 | Fat 17.8g |Sodium 619mg | Carbs 21g | Fiber 1.4g | Sugar 1.8g | Protein 38.4g

Parmesan Pork Chops

Prep Time: 10 minutes.
Cook Time: 15 minutes.
Serves: 4

Ingredients:

- 4 boneless pork chops
- 2 tablespoons olive oil
- ½ cup freshly grated Parmesan
- 1 teaspoon salt
- 1 teaspoon paprika
- 1 teaspoon garlic powder
- 1 teaspoon onion powder
- ½ teaspoon black pepper

Preparation:

1. Pat dry the pork chops with a paper towel and rub them with olive oil.
2. Mix parmesan with spices in a medium bowl.
3. Rub the pork chops with Parmesan mixture.
4. Place 2 seasoned pork chops in each of the two Air Fryer baskets
5. Return the Air Fryer Baskets to the Air Fryer.
6. Choose the Air Fryer mode for Zone 1 with 390 degrees F temperature and 15 minutes cooking time.
7. Select the "MATCH COOK" option to copy the settings for Zone 2.
8. Initiate cooking by pressing the START/PAUSE BUTTON.
9. Flip the pork chops when cooked halfway through, then resume cooking.
10. Serve warm.

Serving Suggestion: Serve boiled rice or steamed cauliflower rice.

Variation Tip: Rub the chops with garlic cloves before seasoning.

Nutritional Information Per Serving:
Calories 396 | Fat 23.2g |Sodium 622mg | Carbs 0.7g | Fiber 0g | Sugar 0g | Protein 45.6g

Beef Cheeseburgers

Prep Time: 15 minutes.
Cook Time: 13 minutes.
Serves: 4

Ingredients:

- 1 lb ground beef
- Salt, to taste
- 2 garlic cloves, minced
- 1 tablespoon soy sauce
- Black pepper, to taste
- 4 American cheese slices
- 4 hamburger buns
- Mayonnaise, to serve
- Lettuce, to serve
- Sliced tomatoes, to serve
- Sliced red onion, to serve

Preparation:

1. Mix beef with soy sauce and garlic in a large bowl.
2. Make 4 patties of 4 inches in diameter.
3. Rub them with salt and black pepper on both sides.
4. Place the 2 patties in each of the Air Fryer baskets.
5. Return the Air Fryer Baskets to the Air Fryer.

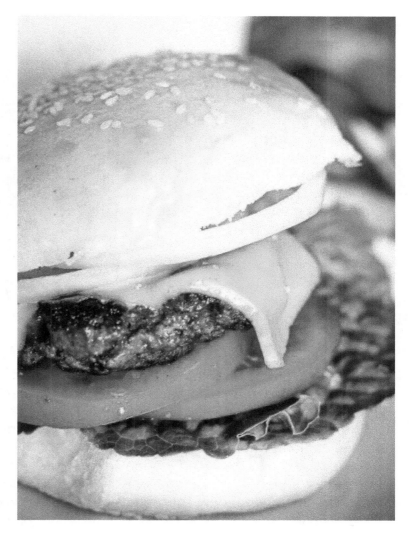

6. Choose the Air Fryer mode for Zone 1 with 390 degrees F temperature and 13 minutes cooking time.
7. Select the "MATCH COOK" option to copy the settings for Zone 2.
8. Initiate cooking by pressing the START/PAUSE BUTTON.
9. Flip each patty once cooked halfway through, and resume cooking.
10. Add each patty to the hamburger buns along with mayo, tomatoes, onions, and lettuce.
11. Serve

Serving Suggestion: Serve with tomato ketchup or chili sauce.

Variation Tip: Add breadcrumbs to the beef burger mixture for a crumbly texture.

Nutritional Information Per Serving:

Calories 437 | Fat 28g |Sodium 1221mg | Carbs 22.3g | Fiber 0.9g | Sugar 8g | Protein 30.3g

Lamb Shank with Mushroom Sauce

Prep Time: 15 minutes.
Cook Time: 35 minutes.
Serves: 4

Ingredients:

- 20 mushrooms, chopped
- 2 red bell pepper, chopped
- 2 red onion, chopped
- 1 cup red wine
- 4 leeks, chopped
- 6 tablespoons balsamic vinegar
- 2 teaspoons black pepper
- 2 teaspoons salt
- 3 tablespoons fresh rosemary
- 6 garlic cloves
- 4 lamb shanks
- 3 tablespoons olive oil

Preparation:

1. Season the lamb shanks with salt, pepper, rosemary, and 1 teaspoon olive oil.
2. Set half of the shanks in each of the Air Fryer baskets.
3. Return the Air Fryer Baskets to the Air Fryer.
4. Choose the Air Fryer mode for Zone 1 with 390 degrees F temperature and 25 minutes cooking time.
5. Select the "MATCH COOK" option to copy the settings for Zone 2.
6. Initiate cooking by pressing the START/PAUSE BUTTON.
7. Flip the shanks halfway through, and resume cooking.
8. Meanwhile, add and heat the remaining olive oil in a skillet.
9. Add onion and garlic to sauté for 5 minutes.
10. Add in mushrooms and cook for 5 minutes.
11. Add red wine and cook until it is absorbed
12. Stir all the remaining vegetables along with black pepper and salt.
13. Cook until vegetables are al dente.
14. Serve the air fried shanks with sautéed vegetable fry.

Serving Suggestion: Serve with sautéed zucchini and green beans.

Variation Tip: Rub the lamb shanks with lemon juice before seasoning.

Nutritional Information Per Serving:
Calories 352 | Fat 9.1g |Sodium 1294mg | Carbs 3.9g | Fiber 1g | Sugar 1g | Protein 61g

Gochujang Brisket

Prep Time: 20 minutes.
Cook Time: 55 minutes.
Serves: 6

Ingredients:

- ½ tablespoons sweet paprika
- ½ teaspoon toasted sesame oil
- 2 lbs beef brisket, cut into 4 pieces
- Salt, to taste
- 1/8 cup Gochujang, Korean chili paste
- Black pepper, to taste
- 1 small onion, diced
- 2 garlic cloves, minced
- 1 teaspoon Asian fish sauce
- 1 ½ tablespoons peanut oil, as needed
- ½ tablespoons fresh ginger, grated
- ¼ teaspoons red chili flakes
- ½ cup of water
- 1 tablespoon ketchup
- 1 tablespoon soy sauce

Preparation:

1. Thoroughly rub the beef brisket with olive oil, paprika, chili flakes, black pepper, and salt.
2. Cut the brisket in half, then divide the beef in the two Air Fryer baskets.
3. Return the Air Fryer Baskets to the Air Fryer.
4. Choose the Air Fryer mode for Zone 1 with 390 degrees F temperature and 35 minutes cooking time.
5. Select the "MATCH COOK" option to copy the settings for Zone 2.
6. Initiate cooking by pressing the START/PAUSE BUTTON.
7. Flip the brisket halfway through, and resume cooking.
8. Meanwhile, heat oil in a skillet and add ginger, onion, and garlic.
9. Sauté for 5 minutes, then add all the remaining ingredients.
10. Cook the mixture for 15 minutes approximately until well thoroughly mixed.
11. Serve the brisket with this sauce on top.

Serving Suggestion: Serve on top of boiled white rice.

Variation Tip: Add Worcestershire sauce and honey to taste.

Nutritional Information Per Serving:
Calories 374 | Fat 25g |Sodium 275mg | Carbs 7.3g | Fiber 0g | Sugar 6g | Protein 12.3g

Chipotle Beef

Prep Time: 15 minutes.
Cook Time: 18 minutes.
Serves: 4

Ingredients:

- 1 lb beef steak, cut into chunks
- 1 large egg
- 1/2 cup parmesan cheese, grated
- 1/2 cup pork panko
- 1/2 teaspoons seasoned salt

Chipotle Ranch Dip

- 1/4 cup mayonnaise
- 1/4 cup sour cream
- 1 teaspoon chipotle paste
- 1/2 teaspoons ranch dressing mix
- 1/4 medium lime, juiced

Preparation:

1. Mix all the ingredients for chipotle ranch dip in a bowl.
2. Keep it in the refrigerator for 30 minutes.
3. Mix pork panko with salt and parmesan.
4. Beat egg in one bowl and spread the panko mixture in another flat bowl.
5. Dip the steak chunks in the egg first, then coat them with panko mixture.
6. Spread them in the two Air fryer baskets and spray them with cooking oil.
7. Return the Air Fryer Baskets to the Air Fryer.
8. Choose the Air Fryer mode for Zone 1 with 390 degrees F temperature and 18 minutes cooking time.
9. Select the "MATCH COOK" option to copy the settings for Zone 2.
10. Initiate cooking by pressing the START/PAUSE BUTTON.
11. Serve with chipotle ranch and salt and pepper on top. Enjoy

Serving Suggestion: Serve with tomato ketchup or chili sauce.

Variation Tip: Add crushed cornflakes for breading to get extra crisp.

Nutritional Information Per Serving:
Calories 310 | Fat 17g |Sodium 271mg | Carbs 4.3g | Fiber 0.9g | Sugar 2.1g | Protein 35g

Zucchini Pork Skewers

Prep Time: 15 minutes.
Cook Time: 23 minutes.
Serves: 4

Ingredients:
- 1 large zucchini, cut 1" pieces
- 1 lb boneless pork belly, cut into cubes
- 1 onion yellow, diced in squares
- 1 ½ cup grape tomatoes
- 1 garlic clove minced
- 1 lemon, juice only
- 1/4 cup olive oil
- 2 tablespoons balsamic vinegar
- 1 teaspoon oregano
- olive oil spray

Preparation:
1. Mix together balsamic vinegar, garlic, oregano lemon juice, and 1/4 cup olive oil in a suitable bowl.
2. Then toss in diced pork pieces and mix well to coat.
3. Leave the seasoned pork to marinate for 60 minutes in the refrigerator.
4. Take suitable wooden skewers for your Air Fryer's Basket, and then thread marinated pork and vegetables on each skewer in an alternating manner.
5. Place half of the skewers in each of the Air fryer baskets and spray them with cooking oil.
6. Return the Air Fryer Baskets to the Air Fryer.
7. Choose the Air Fryer mode for Zone 1 with 390 degrees F temperature and 23 minutes cooking time.
8. Select the "MATCH COOK" option to copy the settings for Zone 2.
9. Initiate cooking by pressing the START/PAUSE BUTTON.
10. Flip the skewers once cooked halfway through, and resume cooking.
11. Serve warm.

Serving Suggestion: Serve with sautéed green beans and cherry tomatoes.
Variation Tip: Use honey glaze to baste the skewers.
Nutritional Information Per Serving:
Calories 459 | Fat 17.7g |Sodium 1516mg | Carbs 1.7g | Fiber 0.5g | Sugar 0.4g | Protein 69.2g

Mustard Rubbed Lamb Chops

Prep Time: 15 minutes.
Cook Time: 31 minutes.
Serves: 4

Ingredients:

- 1 teaspoon Dijon mustard
- 1 teaspoon olive oil
- ½ teaspoon soy sauce
- ½ teaspoon garlic, minced
- ½ teaspoon cumin powder
- ½ teaspoon cayenne pepper
- ½ teaspoon Italian spice blend
- 1/8 teaspoon salt
- 4 pieces of lamb chops

Preparation:

1. Mix Dijon mustard, soy sauce, olive oil, garlic, cumin powder, cayenne pepper, Italian spice blend, and salt in a medium bowl and mix well.
2. Place lamb chops into a Ziploc bag and pour in the marinade.
3. Press the air out of the bag and seal tightly.
4. Press the marinade around the lamb chops to coat.
5. Keep then in the fridge and marinate for at least 30 minutes, up to overnight.
6. Place 2 chops in each of the Air fryer baskets and spray them with cooking oil.
7. Return the Air Fryer Baskets to the Air Fryer.
8. Select the Roast mode for Zone 1 with 350 degrees F temperature and 27 minutes cooking time.
9. Select the "MATCH COOK" option to copy the settings for Zone 2.
10. Initiate cooking by pressing the START/PAUSE BUTTON.
11. Flip the chops once cooked halfway through, and resume cooking.
12. Switch the Air fryer to AIR broil mode and cook for 5 minutes.
13. Serve warm

Serving Suggestion: Serve the chops with a dollop of cream cheese dip on top.

Variation Tip: Rub the lamb chops with balsamic vinegar or honey before seasoning.

Nutritional Information Per Serving:

Calories 264 | Fat 17g |Sodium 129mg | Carbs 0.9g | Fiber 0.3g | Sugar 0g | Protein 27g

Dessert Recipes

Apple Hand Pies

Prep Time: 15 minutes.
Cook Time: 21 minutes.
Serves: 8

Ingredients:

- 8 tablespoons butter, softened
- 12 tablespoons brown sugar
- 2 teaspoons cinnamon, ground
- 4 medium Granny Smith apples, diced
- 2 teaspoons cornstarch
- 4 teaspoons cold water
- 1 (14 oz) package pastry, 9-inch crust pie
- Cooking spray
- 1 tablespoon grapeseed oil
- ½ cup powdered sugar
- 2 teaspoons milk

Preparation:

1. Toss apples with brown sugar, butter, and cinnamon in a suitable skillet.
2. Place the skillet over medium heat and stir cook for 5 minutes.
3. Mix cornstarch with cold water in a small bowl.
4. Add cornstarch mixture into the apple and cook for 1 minute until it thickens.
5. Remove this filling from the heat and allow it to cool.
6. Unroll the pie crust and spray on a floured surface.
7. Cut the dough into 16 equal rectangles.
8. Wet the edges of the 8 rectangles with water and divide the apple filling at the center of these rectangles.
9. Place the other 8 rectangles on top and crimp the edges with a fork, then make 2-3 slashes on top.
10. Place 4 small pies in each of the Air Fryer Baskets.
11. Return the Air Fryer Baskets to the Air Fryer.
12. Choose the Air Fryer mode for Zone 1 with 390 degrees F temperature and 17 minutes cooking time.
13. Select the "MATCH COOK" option to copy the settings for Zone 2.
14. Initiate cooking by pressing the START/PAUSE BUTTON.

15.Flip the pies once cooked halfway through, and resume cooking.
16.Meanwhile, mix sugar with milk.
17.Pour this mixture over the apple pies.
18.Serve fresh.

Serving Suggestion: Serve with apple sauce.

Variation Tip: Add shredded nuts and coconuts to the filling.

Nutritional Information Per Serving:
Calories 284 | Fat 16g |Sodium 252mg | Carbs 31.6g | Fiber 0.9g | Sugar 6.6g | Protein 3.7g

Walnuts Fritters

Prep Time: 15 minutes.
Cook Time: 15 minutes.
Serves: 6

Ingredients:

- 1 cup all-purpose flour
- ½ cup walnuts, chopped
- ¼ cup white sugar
- ¼ cup milk
- 1 egg
- 1 ½ teaspoon baking powder
- 1 pinch salt
- Cooking spray
- 2 tablespoons white sugar
- ½ teaspoon ground cinnamon

Glaze:

- ½ cup confectioners' sugar
- 1 tablespoon milk
- ½ teaspoon caramel extract
- ¼ teaspoons ground cinnamon

Preparation:

1. Layer both Air Fryer Baskets with parchment paper.
2. Grease the parchment paper with cooking spray.
3. Whisk flour with milk, 1/4 cup sugar, egg, baking powder, and salt in a small bowl.
4. Separately mix 2 tablespoons sugar with cinnamon in another bowl, toss in walnuts and mix well to coat.
5. Stir in flour mixture and mix until combined.
6. Drop the fritters mixture using a cookie scoop into the two Air Fryer Baskets.
7. Return the Air Fryer Baskets to the Air Fryer.
8. Choose the Air Fryer mode for Zone 1 with 375 degrees F temperature and 15 minutes cooking time.
9. Select the "MATCH COOK" option to copy the settings for Zone 2.
10. Initiate cooking by pressing the START/PAUSE BUTTON.
11. Flip the fritters once cooked halfway through, then resume cooking.
12. Meanwhile, whisk milk, caramel extract, confectioners' sugar, and cinnamon in a bowl.
13. Transfer fritters to a wire rack and allow them to cool.
14. Drizzle with a glaze over the fritters

Serving Suggestion: Serve with butter pecan ice cream or strawberry jam.

Variation Tip: Add maple syrup on top.

Nutritional Information Per Serving:

Calories 391 | Fat 24g |Sodium 142mg | Carbs 38.5g | Fiber 3.5g | Sugar 21g | Protein 6.6g

Air Fried Bananas

Prep Time: 10 minutes.
Cook Time: 13 minutes.
Serves: 4

Ingredients:

- 4 bananas, sliced
- 1 avocado oil cooking spray

Preparation:

1. Spread the banana slices in the two air fryer baskets in a single layer.
2. Drizzle avocado oil over the banana slices.
3. Return the Air Fryer Baskets to the Air Fryer.
4. Choose the Air Fryer mode for Zone 1 with 350 degrees F temperature and 13 minutes cooking time.
5. Select the "MATCH COOK" option to copy the settings for Zone 2.
6. Initiate cooking by pressing the START/PAUSE BUTTON.
7. Serve

Serving Suggestion: Serve with a dollop of vanilla ice-cream.

Variation Tip: Drizzle chopped nuts on top of the bananas

Nutritional Information Per Serving:
Calories 149 | Fat 1.2g |Sodium 3mg | Carbs 37.6g | Fiber 5.8g | Sugar 29g | Protein 1.1g

Air Fried Beignets

Prep Time: 15 minutes.
Cook Time: 17 minutes.
Serves: 6

Ingredients:

- Cooking spray
- ¼ cup white sugar
- ⅛ cup water
- ½ cup all-purpose flour
- 1 large egg, separated
- 1 ½ teaspoon butter, melted
- ½ teaspoon baking powder
- ½ teaspoon vanilla extract
- 1 pinch salt
- 2 tablespoons confectioners' sugar, or to taste

Preparation:

1. Beat flour with water, sugar, egg yolk, baking powder, butter, vanilla extract, and salt in a large bowl until lumps-free.
2. Beat egg whites in a separate bowl and beat using an electric hand mixer until it forms soft peaks.
3. Add the egg white to the flour batter and mix gently until fully incorporated.
4. Divide the dough into small beignets and place them in the air fryer baskets.
5. Return the Air Fryer Baskets to the Air Fryer.
6. Choose the Air Fryer mode for Zone 1 with 390 degrees F temperature and 17 minutes cooking time.
7. Select the "MATCH COOK" option to copy the settings for Zone 2.
8. Initiate cooking by pressing the START/PAUSE BUTTON.
9. And cook for another 4 minutes. Dust the cooked beignets with sugar.
10. Serve

Serving Suggestion: Serve with a dollop of sweet cream dip

Variation Tip: Add chopped raisins and nuts to the dough.

Nutritional Information Per Serving:
Calories 327 | Fat 14.2g |Sodium 672mg | Carbs 47.2g | Fiber 1.7g | Sugar 24.8g | Protein 4.4g

Biscuit Doughnuts

Prep Time: 15 minutes.
Cook Time: 15 minutes.
Serves: 8

Ingredients:

- ½ cup white sugar
- 1 teaspoon cinnamon
- ½ cup powdered sugar
- 1 can pre-made biscuit dough
- Coconut oil
- Melted butter to brush biscuits

Preparation:

1. Place all the biscuits on a cutting board and cut holes in the center of each biscuit using a cookie cutter.
2. Grease the Air Fryer Baskets with coconut oil.
3. Place the biscuits in the two Air Fryers Baskets while keeping them 1 inch apart.
4. Return the Air Fryer Baskets to the Air Fryer.
5. Choose the Air Fryer mode for Zone 1 with 375 degrees F temperature and 15 minutes cooking time.
6. Select the "MATCH COOK" option to copy the settings for Zone 2.
7. Initiate cooking by pressing the START/PAUSE BUTTON.
8. Brush all the donuts with melted butter and sprinkle cinnamon and sugar on top.
9. Air fry these donuts for one minute more.
10. Enjoy

Serving Suggestion: Serve the doughnuts with chocolate syrup on top.

Variation Tip: Inject strawberry jam into each doughnut.

Nutritional Information Per Serving:
Calories 192 | Fat 9.3g |Sodium 133mg | Carbs 27.1g | Fiber 1.4g | Sugar 19g | Protein 3.2g

Zesty Cranberry Scones

Prep Time: 10 minutes.
Cook Time: 16 minutes.
Serves: 8

Ingredients:

- 4 cups of flour
- 1/2 cup brown sugar
- 2 tablespoons baking powder
- ½ teaspoon ground nutmeg
- ½ teaspoon salt
- ½ cup butter, chilled and diced
- 2 cups fresh cranberry
- 2/3 cup sugar
- 2 tablespoons orange zest
- 1 ¼ cup half and half cream
- 2 eggs

Preparation:

1. Whisk flour with baking powder, salt, nutmeg, and both the sugars in a bowl.
2. Stir in egg and cream, mix well to form a smooth dough.
3. Fold in cranberries along with the orange zest.
4. Knead this dough well on a work surface.
5. Cut 3-inch circles out of the dough.
6. Divide the scones in the Air Fryer Baskets and spray them with cooking oil.
7. Return the Air Fryer Baskets to the Air Fryer.
8. Choose the Air Fryer mode for Zone 1 with 375 degrees F temperature and 16 minutes cooking time.
9. Select the "MATCH COOK" option to copy the settings for Zone 2.
10. Initiate cooking by pressing the START/PAUSE BUTTON.
11. Flip the scones once cooked halfway and resume cooking.
12. Enjoy

Serving Suggestion: Serve with cranberry jam on the side.

Variation Tip: Add raisins instead of cranberries to the dough.

Nutritional Information Per Serving:
Calories 204 | Fat 9g |Sodium 91mg | Carbs 27g | Fiber 2.4g | Sugar 15g | Protein 1.3g

Apple Nutmeg Flautas

Prep Time: 10 minutes.
Cook Time: 8 minutes.
Serves: 8

Ingredients:

- ¼ cup light brown sugar
- 1/8 cup all-purpose flour
- ¼ teaspoons ground cinnamon
- Nutmeg, to taste
- 4 apples, peeled, cored & sliced
- ½ lemon, juice, and zest
- 6 (10-inch) flour tortillas
- Vegetable oil
- Caramel sauce
- Cinnamon sugar

Preparation:

1. Mix brown sugar with cinnamon, nutmeg, and flour in a large bowl.
2. Toss in apples in lemon juice. Mix well.
3. Place a tortilla at a time on a flat surface and add ½ cup of the apple mixture to the tortilla.
4. Roll the tortilla into a burrito and seal it tightly and hold it in place with a toothpick.
5. Repeat the same steps with the remaining tortillas and apple mixture.
6. Place two apple burritos in each of the Air Fryer Baskets and spray them with cooking oil.
7. Return the Air Fryer Baskets to the Air Fryer.
8. Choose the Air Fryer mode for Zone 1 with 400 degrees F temperature and 8 minutes cooking time.
9. Select the "MATCH COOK" option to copy the settings for Zone 2.
10. Initiate cooking by pressing the START/PAUSE BUTTON.
11. Flip the burritos once cooked halfway through, then resume cooking.
12. Garnish with caramel sauce and cinnamon sugar.
13. Enjoy

Serving Suggestion: Serve with maple syrup on the side.

Variation Tip: Add orange juice and zest for change of taste.

Nutritional Information Per Serving:
Calories 157 | Fat 1.3g |Sodium 27mg | Carbs 1.3g | Fiber 1g | Sugar 2.2g | Protein 8.2g

Apple Crisp

Prep Time: 15 minutes.
Cook Time: 14 minutes.
Serves: 8

Ingredients:

- 3 cups apples, chopped
- 1 tablespoon pure maple syrup
- 2 teaspoons lemon juice
- 3 tablespoons all-purpose flour
- 1/3 cup quick oats
- ¼ cup brown sugar
- 2 tablespoons light butter, melted
- ½ teaspoon cinnamon

Preparation:

1. Toss the chopped apples with 1 tablespoon of all-purpose flour, cinnamon, maple syrup, and lemon juice in a suitable bowl.
2. Divide the apples in the two air fryer baskets with their crisper plates.
3. Whisk oats, brown sugar, and remaining all-purpose flour in a small bowl.
4. Stir in melted butter, then divide this mixture over the apples.
5. Return the Air Fryer Baskets to the Air Fryer.
6. Select the Bake mode for Zone 1 with 375 degrees F temperature and 14 minutes cooking time.
7. Select the "MATCH COOK" option to copy the settings for Zone 2.
8. Initiate cooking by pressing the START/PAUSE BUTTON.
9. Enjoy fresh

Serving Suggestion: Serve with a warming cup of hot chocolate.

Variation Tip: Use crushed cookies or graham crackers instead of oats.

Nutritional Information Per Serving:
Calories 258 | Fat 12.4g |Sodium 79mg | Carbs 34.3g | Fiber 1g | Sugar 17g | Protein 3.2g

Oreo Rolls

Prep Time: 10 minutes.
Cook Time: 8 minutes.
Serves: 9

Ingredients:

- 1 crescent sheet roll
- 9 Oreo cookies
- Cinnamon powder, to serve
- Powdered sugar, to serve

Preparation:

1. Spread the crescent sheet roll and cut it into 9 equal squares.
2. Place one cookie at the center of each square.
3. Wrap each square around the cookies and press the ends to seal.
4. Place half of the wrapped cookies in each air fryer basket.
5. Return the Air Fryer Baskets to the Air Fryer.
6. Select the Bake mode for Zone 1 with 360 degrees F temperature and 4-6 minutes cooking time.
7. Select the "MATCH COOK" option to copy the settings for Zone 2.
8. Initiate cooking by pressing the START/PAUSE BUTTON.
9. Check for the doneness of the cookie rolls if they are golden brown, else cook 1-2 minutes more.
10. Garnish the rolls with sugar and cinnamon.
11. Serve.

Serving Suggestion: Serve a cup of spice latte or hot chocolate.

Variation Tip: Dip the rolls in melted chocolate for a change of taste.

Nutritional Information Per Serving:
Calories 175 | Fat 13.1g |Sodium 154mg | Carbs 14g | Fiber 0.8g | Sugar 8.9g | Protein 0.7g

3-weeks Meal Plan

Week 1

Monday

Breakfast: Morning Patties

Lunch: Sweet Potatoes with Honey Butter

Snack: Fried Olives

Dinner: Mustard Rubbed Lamb Chops

Dessert: Walnuts Fritters

Tuesday

Breakfast: Crispy Hash Browns

Lunch: Air Fried Okra

Snack: Crispy Plantain Chips

Dinner: Zucchini Pork Skewers

Dessert: Apple Hand Pies

Wednesday

Breakfast: Air Fried Sausage

Lunch: Quinoa Patties

Snack: Peppered Asparagus

Dinner: Chipotle Beef

Dessert: Air Fried Bananas

Thursday

Breakfast: Pepper Egg Cups

Lunch: Zucchini Cakes

Snack: Cauliflower Gnocchi

Dinner: Gochujang Brisket

Dessert: Air Fried Beignets

Friday

Breakfast: Breakfast Bacon

Lunch: Saucy Carrots

Snack: Fried Halloumi Cheese

Dinner: Lamb Shank with Mushroom Sauce

Dessert: Biscuit Doughnuts

Saturday

Breakfast: Biscuit Balls

Lunch: Falafel

Snack: Crispy Tortilla Chips

Dinner: Beef Cheeseburgers

Dessert: Zesty Cranberry Scones

Sunday

Breakfast: Morning Egg Rolls

Lunch: Lime Glazed Tofu

Snack: Parmesan French Fries

Dinner: Parmesan Pork Chops

Dessert: Apple Nutmeg Flautas

Week 2

Monday:

Breakfast: Spinach Egg Muffins

Lunch: Chicken Drumettes

Snack: Chicken Crescent Wraps

Dinner: Pork Chops with Broccoli

Dessert: Apple Crisp

Tuesday

Breakfast: Pumpkin Muffins

Lunch: General Tso's Chicken

Snack: Chicken Stuffed Mushrooms

Dinner: Turkey and Beef Meatballs

Dessert: Oreo Rolls

Wednesday

Breakfast: Cinnamon Toasts

Lunch: Bang-Bang Chicken

Snack: Onion Rings

Dinner: Pork Chops with Brussels Sprouts

Dessert: Apple Nutmeg Flautas

Thursday

Breakfast: Morning Patties

Lunch: Bacon-Wrapped Chicken

Snack: Potato Tater Tots

Dinner: Air Fryer Meatloaves

Dessert: Apple Crisp

Friday

Breakfast: Crispy Hash Browns

Lunch: Crumbed Chicken Katsu

Snack: Crispy Plantain Chips

Dinner: Pork with Green Beans and Potatoes

Dessert: Oreo Rolls

Saturday

Breakfast: Air Fried Sausage

Lunch: Breaded Scallops

Snack: Peppered Asparagus

Dinner: Veggie Stuffed Chicken Breasts

Dessert: Apple Hand Pies

Sunday

Breakfast: Pepper Egg Cups

Lunch: Salmon Nuggets

Snack: Cauliflower Gnocchi

Dinner: Cheddar- Stuffed Chicken

Dessert: Walnuts Fritters

Week 3

Monday:

Breakfast: Breakfast Bacon

Lunch: Crispy Catfish

Snack: Fried Halloumi Cheese

Dinner: Balsamic Duck Breast

Dessert: Air Fried Bananas

Tuesday

Breakfast: Biscuit Balls

Lunch: Crusted Tilapia

Snack: Crispy Tortilla Chips

Dinner: Brazilian Chicken Drumsticks

Dessert: Air Fried Beignets

Wednesday

Breakfast: Morning Egg Rolls

Lunch: Glazed Scallops

Snack: Parmesan French Fries

Dinner: Chili Chicken Wings

Dessert: Biscuit Doughnuts

Thursday

Breakfast: Spinach Egg Muffins

Lunch: Crusted Cod

Snack: Chicken Crescent Wraps

Dinner: Air Fried Turkey Breast

Dessert: Zesty Cranberry Scones

Friday

Breakfast: Pumpkin Muffins

Lunch: Savory Salmon Fillets

Snack: Chicken Stuffed Mushrooms

Dinner: Chicken Potatoes

Dessert: Apple Nutmeg Flautas

Saturday

Breakfast: Morning Patties

Lunch: Salmon with Fennel Salad

Snack: Onion Rings

Dinner: Pickled Chicken Fillets

Dessert: Apple Crisp

Sunday

Breakfast: Crispy Hash Browns

Lunch: Buttered Mahi Mahi

Snack: Potato Tater Tots

Dinner: Crusted Chicken Breast

Dessert: Oreo Rolls

Conclusion

It's about time that you give these 2 baskets air fryer recipes a try and surprise your family and loved ones with their great flavor and super crispy texture. In this cookbook, we have tried to introduce you to the recent hit of the air frying technology, the Ninja 2 baskets Air fryer, and brought you all the basic and easy to start with recipes that will help you create a complete menu of your own or you can use the three weeks plan given in this book.

The "two basket air fryers" have come as an amazing surprise for all those who always wanted to cook a variety of meals at the time and save some time. Now with this air fryer, a person can use two different chambers at a time- each of them having 4 qt volume for cooking. Or a user can simply sync them together to get an 8 qt capacity. Isn't that amazing? Now cooking large and small serving portions is not a problem as long as you have this Air fryer at home.

Ninja Foodi, due to its effective dual chamber heating technology and amazing design, has upgraded the air frying landscape, and it is now giving major competition to all its Air Fryer competitors in the market. Not only this air fryer provides two chambers to cook as much food you want to cook, but it is extremely user friendly as well. You can sync the two baskets to cook at the same time and temperature, or you can use them as separate independent chambers to cook different meals at the same time.

So, if you haven't yet tried the two-basket Air Fryer or are still getting a grasp at this technology, then this cookbook is the right fit for you! You have all the luscious meals along with a three weeks meal plan to prepare all sorts of meat cuts, vegetarian entrees, snacks, desserts, and breakfast in just a few minutes. So, don't wait around; put on your aprons, and pick your favorite recipe from this book and do some air frying!